Who's Being Served?

Who's Being Served?

Placing Students at the Center of Their Learning Experiences

John M. Hayward

ROWMAN & LITTLEFIELD
Lanham • Boulder • New York • London

Published by Rowman & Littlefield
A wholly owned subsidiary of The Rowman & Littlefield Publishing Group, Inc.
4501 Forbes Boulevard, Suite 200, Lanham, Maryland 20706
www.rowman.com

Unit A, Whitacre Mews, 26-34 Stannary Street, London SE11 4AB

British Library Cataloguing in Publication Information Available

Library of Congress Cataloging-in-Publication Data Available

ISBN 9781475841275 (hardback : alk. paper) | ISBN 9781475841282 (pbk. : alk. paper) | ISBN 9781475841299 (electronic)

∞ ™ The paper used in this publication meets the minimum requirements of American National Standard for Information Sciences Permanence of Paper for Printed Library Materials, ANSI/NISO Z39.48-1992.

Printed in the United States of America

To Virginia
and other teachers like her
who entered the profession to answer a calling to serve

Contents

Preface

People who are not in education like to believe the summer months for teachers are unfair, worry-free stress breaks, but that is not true. After twelve months' worth of work gets packed into nine months of time, teachers need some relief from the exhaustion. Planning activities, implementing and adjusting lesson plans, using underresourced and therefore self-purchased or created materials, and assessing student mastery of necessary skills wear on teachers—even if they are trained, degreed, and experienced.

Preparing for the school year can start as soon as the previous year ends. Putting away supplies inspires ways the next lesson can be improved, and before you know it, there goes summer.

For many teachers, back-to-school dreams begin in late July. What should be pleasant, restful summer evenings somehow turn overnight into panicked early-morning wakings of wondering why nightmares about empty bulletin boards and unruly students would even be on one's mind at this time. *I should be sleeping! Why am I dreaming about not having enough photocopies made or the Internet connection failing during an official observation?*

Then August begins.

Teachers anticipate their first day ever or dust off what was packed away at the end of spring and plug themselves into preparation mode. They ask, *What worked before, and what can I do again? What should I not repeat? Where will I find inspirational ideas to reach my most challenging students?* This equipping process includes gathering resources from anything offering something new.

Well, teachers and administrators, this book *is* that something new.

Within these pages are the field-tested creative sparks and researched strategies for putting students at the center of their own learning experience. Better-prepared and confident teachers create environments for prepared and confident students. In fact, these are the teachers more likely to risk letting go of control and letting students direct paths to their own learning.

In between planning, grading, reporting, decorating, constructing, counseling, and the numerous other roles there are to play as a teacher or an administrator, consult this text for ways to reset the balance and put more aspects of education into the hands of the investors and consumers.

Ownership, responsibility, the chance to risk, fail, and safely recover are what students want; they will say so if you ask them. Now is the time to be the aware, transparent, and ultimately fulfilled (not exhausted) teacher you entered this profession to become.

Putting students first does not require more work; it requires *smarter* work.

These chapters make multiple references to the restaurant model of understanding classroom design and instructional delivery. If you think about it, the two environments have a lot in common. As teachers welcome students to their seats each year, it helps to know what to serve and how to keep the business afloat. Just like the owners of a unique restaurant, teachers and administrators want to keep customers coming back for more and help them feel inspired to create some things on their own.

In your renewed, student-centered approach, you will be raising a new generation of students who hunger for and live, not just receive, their learning opportunities. These are the world-changers ready for the diverse challenges their future will present, and both you and your students will learn a lot in the process.

Acknowledgments

A classroom is one of the closest and neediest mission fields ever. I must credit God first for developing this calling to teach students wherever they are and to help them achieve their best. The creative ideas and insights bearing my name, the patience to slow down and see student needs, and the compassion that inspires me to get out of bed and into a school every morning are all his doing.

To Tom Koerner, vice president and education editor at Rowman & Littlefield, for reaching out to me weeks after my *Educational Leadership* article appeared. His encouragement to get writing helped me fill these pages in the months that followed.

To Naperville Community School District 203, whose support has fostered an environment of safe risk and discovery for me since I arrived there in 1999. Even though I would not trade my years in private schools or my second career as an adjunct writing instructor for anything, District 203 is a place I am happy to call home. To the administrators and staff, fellow teachers, students, and parents whose friendly interaction and trust has produced the environment where these ideas bounce and often land successfully, thank you.

To Mike Doman, Jackie Thornton, Dr. Lynn Andrees, Nicki Weiss, and Megan Plackett, who accommodate impromptu drive-by, idea-sharing sessions, thanks for listening and sharpening the craft. We are think-partners, and I am thankful we share the same crazy brain. Cathy Gottlieb, my fellow Learning Commons director, you have taught me so much about how the capital city of literacy operates. Thank you for your patience, leadership, and shared office space. Do I have a desk yet?

To Brian and Kelly Herkert, who believed me when I suggested their path to opening a soup and sandwich shop mirrored that of teachers preparing a classroom. We have more in common than we thought! On the cold November afternoon when I went to Everdine's Grilled Cheese Company to interview you, the tomato soup really did taste like home.

To former students, from the young and near to the older and more seasoned world-changers, thank you for teaching me. Though I may not instantly recall your name if we meet face-to-face, I will remember exactly where you sat. Please keep in touch so I can read the continuing chapters of your life story.

To my family, close and extended, who have endured volumes of teacher stories, counseled years of fatigue and complaints, and celebrated many misty-eyed breakthroughs. See? It was all worth it.

Introduction

In 2015, I responded to an invitation to submit a piece to *Educational Leadership* magazine on why teachers should put relationships first. Preparing content and delivering instruction matters more when students know they are valued, right? I believe this, act upon it with each year's new roster of students in my classes, and learn new things in this area all the time.

Could an opportunity to reach teachers with encouraging information about the difference putting relationships first makes help change education from teacher centered to student centered? In my hopes, I started writing.

Assembling more than twenty years of experiences into an article proved difficult at first. I have taught teenagers and adults in two states and four schools representing both private and public education. How could I choose what failures to expose and what advice to include? After a few weeks of organizing and redrafting, I settled my words into a manageable form for submission.

The article, titled "Classrooms That Put People First," appeared in the September 2016 issue and addressed how to create a happy and safe learning environment for students. As more teachers read the article, their feedback confirmed the necessity of keeping relationship building at the forefront of school culture.

A few weeks after the article appeared, I received an offer to extend relationships-first strategies into a full-length text. What you hold now is the book expressing that core message for teachers and administrators: students matter. Getting to know who they are, hearing their stories, and identifying their dreams or fears helps smooth the path for facilitating lifelong learning. The humble yet inspiring mission to engage their impressionable minds re-starts every day. Perhaps today is when your path toward student-centered instruction can continue or begin.

Each chapter of this book develops the idea that classrooms have much in common with restaurants in how successful preparation and delivery focus on the customer. The culinary and service industry references make sense when you consider how much planning, observation, and personalized work teachers invest on behalf of their students. From anticipating opening day to reflecting on the end of a term, the parallels between the two environments remain strong.

This book offers welcome advice and presents many thoughts to ponder. The questions you encounter throughout the book—whether at the end of each chapter or within—are ones all educators need to address individually and in their community. In fact, the length and meaning of the book doubles when you answer the questions for yourself, among your professional learning community members, or with a book club.

Whatever suggestions I provide come not only from experience but also from a hope that you will achieve similar success with your learners in your environment. May your discussions about this book inspire improvements that lead to lasting change.

Those who put relationships first yield the greater reward for their professional and personal lives, creating, in the end, the kinds of schools and types of students we have wanted and needed all along. There has been enough talk about the problem with today's schools. When we engage in the conversation about keeping students at the center of their learning experience, we make great strides toward a solution.

Chapter One

Setting the Table

Preparing the Learning Environment for Greatness

PREPPING THE ROOM FOR OPENING DAY

Educators can learn a lot about preparation from restaurants. A truly amazing and memorable dining experience does not occur without just the right balance and appeal. Lighting, music, preparation, presentation, and service must be executed with precision and sensitivity. None of this happens without some exploration into what makes a great restaurant business and dining environment. Compare figures 1.1 and 1.2 and note the similarities.

Perhaps consultants have been brought in to scout out the perfect restaurant location and layout. Dieticians may influence the final menu. The furniture must be functional yet comfortable and inviting. Lighting needs to be cozy while also balancing safety and visibility. The decor must contribute to the sense of comfort and not intrude upon patron sensitivity. Service, if not well trained and executed, can turn away customers and cause a devastating reputation to ripple across town in no time.

Think about your most pleasurable dining experience. Did you question the plushness of the seating? Did you note how the lighting and the music had been dimmed to the perfect levels? These essential factors may not even have registered in your awareness; they were the background to your primary focus on the food and the company you came to enjoy. What made this possible? Research, planning, and observation.

The owner and manager of a new establishment invest countless hours before the diners first arrive to make sure every element is just right. When the doors open and customers take their seats, most of the foundational work has been done. Minor adjustments can be made at any time, but not drastic

Figure 1.1. An empty but prepared restaurant awaits patrons. ***pixabay***

ones without causing a mid-meal disruption. Lights are securely placed, surfaces are dusted, supplies and provisions are fully stocked, and every possible scenario has been rehearsed. Customers have had little to do but anticipate two of the most critical factors in the whole process: choice and satisfaction.

The analogy between restaurant and classroom is now complete. Schools prepare a space for consumers whose critical and informed choices propel or hinder success. Preparation and delivery are essential yet meaningless without addressing the needs of the patrons.

Oh, and there will be critics, from the wise to the opinionated, highlighting the most insignificant details. Every office, classroom, hallway, bulletin board, and, yes, even the restroom, can make or break the engagement level of a guest. No wonder the planning never ends!

Before the tables get set to deliver five-star instruction, consider the environment in which the students will be most productive, confident, and engaged. How much choice are students offered? Do they walk away satisfied? Will the offerings one day leave them hungry for more the next day? Changes cannot wait until next year.

Do you go to students, ask how they are doing and what they would like customized for their tastes? Servers do. If a student does not understand something, don't move ahead or away. Come back, lean in, and discover

Figure 1.2. An empty but equipped classroom waits for students. ***pixabay***

what that something is. Be the winner of the customer service award through listening, attending, and providing. When students see their teacher doing those three things, they will reciprocate.

CREATING AN ENVIRONMENT CONDUCIVE TO LEARNING

Learning occurs best in an environment created, maintained, and reevaluated by and for students. Answers to what belongs in a learning space will, and should, vary. No one design or layout will work for what is ultimately a very diverse audience. What visitors and patrons of a learning space see should be what the community values. Do the walls celebrate and encourage creativity? Are the resources on display actually going to be used frequently throughout the school year? Can students learn and work in more than one pose and location? (See chapter 4 for activity ideas related to productive classroom movement.)

Careful observations reveal how students focus better in an uncluttered and less-busy space. How can one expect students to attend to the instructor or to the front of the room when the walls themselves are distracting? Sure, one might think being saturated in a busy environment would train or instill the skill of tuning everything else out, but that is not always the case. Just because a teacher can grade papers in a coffee shop, waiting room, busy home, or (gasp) a professional development conference among other distractions does not mean everyone should.

Teachers fight a daily battle to get students' attention. From where is the competition coming? Technology such as tablets or phones and fidget devices, be they spinners or other handheld objects, are not always to blame. When the decorations on the walls are busier than the learners are, something needs to give. When every inch of the classroom is cluttered with posters and pictures, so is the mind trying to filter those distractors out in order to find the essentials. Perhaps the one wall to fill should be the one *behind* the students.

Should you display student work? Absolutely celebrate student creations and accomplishments, but whose work will make the cut if not every piece will fit? If a student's work isn't on the wall, why would that student look there more than once? A resource wall would be a good option once in a while: a place for instructions and reminders about specific and commonly confused skills.

Do students themselves participate in classroom decor? Of all the wonderful, exciting choices students get to make in your learning space, could one of them be how to complete the design of the room itself to meet their needs, satisfy their tastes, and reflect their wonderful diversity? How much more engaged and comfortable (and safe) would students feel if the room reflected their cultures, backgrounds, and interests? Color scheme, furniture, lighting—ask students for their input.

Exemplars of student work, motivational posters, and policy pages are not the teacher's only display options. Can students personalize the space with one item from home? Could teachers reduce anxiety and boost confidence with something as simple as room design? Discover this balance together; own it and celebrate it.

SETTING THE TABLE

The steps one takes to prepare a restaurant or to prepare a classroom are nearly identical. Throughout most of 2016, Brian and Kelly Herkert worked out the details of what would make their new concept restaurant the best one around. Everdine's Grilled Cheese Company in downtown Naperville, Illinois, now specializes in thick-sliced, deliciously original sandwiches, but their opening day, Kelly says, was pushed back almost nine months. Of all the concerns they could invest in before opening their doors, the top two were the layout of the floor plan and the menu.

"We brought in a consultant to help us convert the previous tenant's arrangement," Kelly recalls. "Moving plumbing for the kitchen and restrooms was the most challenging and costly part, but we had to; the former plan wasn't going to work for us." Brian and Kelly also made several adjustments to their workspace, even after opening, once they realized how the traffic flow of grillers, cashiers, and staff influenced efficiency. "Moving our product from the prep space to the counter is critical without bumping into other people or risking dropping what you've made and having to start over," Kelly explains. "The current layout works for us, but we wouldn't have known that without trying different plans. In fact, we did a lot of experimenting and research, which is why opening got pushed back."

The Herkerts adjusted the menu based on customer feedback and seasonal tastes. An egg salad sandwich with bacon and grilled cheese, for example, did not sell well in the colder months, so it was removed. "We were preparing but not using so much egg salad that it became obvious people did not want this in the winter," Kelly concedes. "Maybe we will bring it back in the spring. And our homemade chili, which is popular in the winter, will probably give way to more brothy soups in the summer . . . or salads."

The original vision for the menu included over fifty options, but the Herkerts soon realized this was too much and just wasn't practical. Customers today can easily read the eleven sandwich options available at any given time on the restaurant's large chalkboard menu. Next to it, another smaller board details the soups and sides. Creative names for sandwiches draw interest in their ingredients like the Al Pa-cheeso, Tuna Turner, the '81 Caprice Classic, or the Turkey Meltdown. Brian specializes in making all the soups from scratch in the back kitchen, so everything tastes fresh, not canned or reheated.

One favorite menu option is the "Build Your Own" sandwich, on which a customer can include any combination of seven cheeses, seven meats, or twelve veggies. Those are a lot of choices!

When asked what research, planning, and observation they conducted in the time before opening, Kelly confesses to doing some menu hunting. "Brian and I would walk into other restaurants and check out things like the decor, the menu, the prep line setup and the atmosphere. We looked at photos on Yelp to see if pictures and comments matched the patron experience." Even though the couple has restaurant preparation and management experience, a little extra research helped.

In the months and then the nervous hours before opening, the focus was always on the customers, Kelly says. "I was both excited and scared to open that door, but eleven o'clock came and people were already lined up down the sidewalk. We didn't advertise, not even to our friends at first, but word got out, and there they were."

"Looking back, it was the scariest thing we've ever done. It took us three days to work everything out. I had a sign that said, 'This might take a little while. Thank you for your patience.' It was craziness, but it takes time. It's probably the same thing with school."

This is where the most significant parallels between the classroom and the restaurant become obvious. Reread this section and translate each experience Kelly shares in the context of preparing a workspace, curriculum, activities, and assessments for incoming students in a school. Choice, flexibility, observation, assessment, and adaptations are all part of success whether one is planning meals or lessons.

The nervous excitement Brian and Kelly felt leading up to the first day is something every teacher, staff member, and administrator *should* feel. Conversations with others in their professional community, observations of how other restaurants worked, and flexible adaptations to their overall plan (from workflow to product) contributed to the success of the Herkerts' business. Those in education need to do the same.

SUPPLIES!

Properly equipping the student-centered environment is also important. Through networking opportunities, learn where to get good classroom materials. Teacher supply stores often have membership incentives, tax-exempt offers, and special sales in August. Find a local donation center to give what is no longer in use and pick up what has potential, or perhaps establish a common table somewhere in the school building for a leave one/take one supply exchange.

Repurposing anything is a wise, money-saving strategy upon which teachers thrive. Turn last year's manila folders inside out for another year's use. Cut unused "nonsensitive" handouts in half and reuse as scratch paper for list making or note taking. All left-behind writing utensils become next year's available stock (wrap the icky ones with decorative duct tape). Find ways to reimagine items to meet daily needs; this will save money and model frugal, green practices as well.

Even items around the house can be drafted into service. That ugly coffee mug becomes the room's extra pen and pencil holder. The standing paper towel rack that only took up counter space in the kitchen will make an excellent toilet paper roll holder for the back of the room near the garbage can. Seriously, never buy boxed tissues. A six-dollar, twelve-roll pack of toilet paper ("round tissues") will last a full year and students will not care. A teacher's limited funds have better places to go than to dress up something that holds mucus for a few seconds and then gets tossed in the garbage.

Resist the temptation to offer extra credit to students who bring in supplies. The grade book is a reflection of academic skills and a balance sheet of mastery. Going to the store is not an opportunity everyone sees equally and should not influence grades in any manner. Let students know that contributing to the class supply is a welcome help, especially for consumables, but that not doing so will not be punished. Students' creative vision for how to accessorize will truly make the classroom theirs as well. Consider an advertisement at the open house for what you and your students have discovered would be useful—within reason, of course. Some teachers (ahem) have had to go without their disco ball, beanbag chairs, and shag carpeting for more than twenty years now.

STEPPING BACK

The end of the last day before students arrive is more a time of reflection than preparation. Trust that the work invested so far will be sufficient. Do not second guess. Take comfort in knowing that the more real teachers are, the more students will learn to be authentic as well. The more stressed, nervous, or aggressive teachers are, the more upset students become.

Although students do not like to show it, especially as they get into the late teen years, they really do enjoy going to school. The pressure becomes one of image and fitting in, which unfairly intrudes upon a natural love everyone has—that is to discover, learn, and apply new skills. Tap into this curiosity for learning and fewer eyes will be on hair, shoes, and accessories. Instead, students will be looking into deeper things, such as how to collaborate to solve problems, how to overcome challenges to meet a valued need, or how to break out of a cycle of fixed thinking in a discipline and experience true success.

Before the doors open for business, a restaurant manager might look back one more time, finger on the light switch, admiring all the tables perfectly dressed for the next day's event. A teacher might turn back at the door after having moved thirty desks into five different arrangements and tearing down or stapling up wall displays. But eventually, one reaches the point of knowing there is nothing more to do. Tomorrow starts a new day. Go home and get some good sleep. You're going to need it.

CHAPTER 1 FOOD FOR THOUGHT

What floor plan, lesson plan, assessment, and design choices will students have the freedom to make in your class?

____

____

How will you and students contribute to and measure the success of class culture? If needed, how will that collaboration make adjustments to the class culture?

Why, despite all of your preparations for the classroom, is it essential for students also to contribute to the construction of their physical learning environment?

This fed my thinking:

I am hungry to pursue or try:

Chapter Two

This Classroom Is Open for Business!

OPEN THE DOOR AND LET THEM IN

Since you were not nervous the night before, you will not be as anxious the next morning. Your power outfit, what you feel best wearing, is all ready to go. In fact, you have been picturing yourself wearing this in front of your classroom for a few weeks already. All your back-to-school dreams included clothing, right? You are not *that* unprepared.

Because you ate a balanced breakfast, you will have fuel to get you through the morning. Arriving at school just a little early lets you settle your own nerves and catch up with coworkers. Have a collegial conversation or two. Chat it up, but be careful not to engage in any doubt talk. Attitudes are as highly contagious in this setting as they are before a test or a big game. Today's big game is meeting your students, getting to know them, and introducing them to you, the environment, and the goals.

While most people know first impressions are valuable, the frequency of teacher and student interactions allows for many do-overs. Students will need second chances on many issues throughout their academic careers, which affords the teacher some as well. Modeling an honest transparency lets students know that even if they make mistakes, there is a path to navigate toward redemption. This mind-set takes the edge off first-day perfection and makes it fun instead. Maybe you should set aside a power outfit for day two just in case.

ACCLIMATE AND DISCOVER

At Everdine's, the current layout of kitchen equipment is not what it looked like on opening day. The chaos of trying to serve customers fresh soup and a steaming grilled cheese sandwich while crossing paths with other staff negatively affected the overall experience. Only a few days in, Brian and Kelly knew something needed to change. They rehearsed the ideal flow from order to completion aloud with pantomimed gestures. Though it took some time to rearrange each appliance and accessory, the staff gained efficiency, morale, and even counter space.

"So much better now," Kelly confesses with an experienced sigh of recollection.

Minor adjustments will occur in your classroom on the fly. You did not know that Jimmy has light sensitivity and prefers to sit away from the windows. No one told you that over the summer Amber started going out with Robyn's ex-boyfriend (who thankfully is in another class), so monitoring their interactions will require more care. You had Manny sitting in the middle of three desks, but you see now that his right arm is in a sling and a seat on the far side near an open aisle would be better so he is not crowded.

Do you see how you could not have planned for these issues? So why worry? The dictatorial model of classroom management can disintegrate in the first few seconds, so do not bother with the overlord act. Oppositional differences might make you feel good and power rich, but if it comes at the expense of the learner's comfort, you have already lost. Back down, be yourself, and try the change in plans. This fragile first-day relationship-building process sets the tone for the rest of the day, which influences the week and so on.

Think of students' comfort as they enter your space. You know from experience that restaurant staff will attempt to accommodate a patron's request, within reason.

"Can we have a booth instead of a center table?"

"Can you bring me a new coffee mug? This one is dirty."

"Can you close the blinds, please? The sun is in our eyes."

Yet you still use discernment when fielding student seat requests. To the student rushing to secure a seat in the back row, you whisper so no one else can hear, "No, you may not move to the back of the room; your learning plan states that preferential seating close to the front of the room is best for you. Let me show you some choices over here." Since this moment highlights the delicate balance of your room/my room, take time to usher students in with care and offer the limited, yet good, options from which they may choose.

A student's seat is a temporary home. Comfort matters, and placement can be pleasing or punishing. Ever had a restaurant table next to the bathroom or right near the entrance? Location can enhance or ruin the whole experience. Your teacher station, whether you have a desk, table, or just a corner, has not gone untouched without some personalized modifications, has it? Let students get acquainted with what is going to be the place from which they share, volunteer, take risks, and listen. What students choose in this moment already says a lot about them, so let them choose their own seats while you observe how it works out.

Students in the back will not be able to avoid you; if you roam throughout the room, you eliminate a true "front" to the learning space. Barriers need not be physical to maintain a respectful balance between adult and learner, so break down the invisible curtain between the front and back of the room. Help each student feel included by naturally moving to every corner and angle. Your best observations will be made from these locations. Communicate with your body language your ability to approach each student non-threateningly and you will model that this space is shared and respected.

DAY ONE: GETTING TO KNOW YOU

What would happen if students did *not* get a syllabus on the first day of class but engaged in bell-to-bell activities that built community and valued relationships instead? You have the rest of the year to talk curriculum. Today is the best chance you have to meet the people in front of you and let them get to know you. The course content is important but not of more value than the people you will ask to be engaged in it for the next semester or two.

The safety and joy students will experience in your room gets its start in these first critical moments. Students who insist on a syllabus may have one, of course, for their own interest or their parents' curiosity. You simply may not go over it until day two.

Teachers should never lay down the law or bully their way into earning respect. This transaction of trust is something you first give away and then harvest in return. Day one is a little about you and a whole lot about them (you are outnumbered, after all). Students will not care about the coursework until they know their teacher genuinely cares about them. One way to show this is in the getting-to-know-you phase of introductions.

If we expect transparency and openness from our students, we need to be humble and model the same things ourselves. An icebreaker activity like a simple question-and-answer session breaks down defenses of self-preservation and invites a sense of warmth and security missing in so many adolescent lives. Your classroom is like a safe house on their path, and since you are the host, your ability to demonstrate compassion matters. Dedicate the whole first day to relationship building.

Taking attendance probably has to come first, but there is a way to have some fun with it. Start at the bottom of the roster and work your way up. For the whole rest of the day, as it has been for years, the Z kid will be waiting and waiting for his or her name to be called. In your class, this child will be first. The A kid has always been first. Perspective is a valuable, teachable trait! This also lets students know you can see things from alternate views—you are flexible and creative.

Ask students how they pronounce their names specifically and repeat it back to them until you have it right. This patience reveals your interest in your students. The dry roll call just to see if anyone is absent disregards the beautiful, talented people inhabiting those names. Make notes on the roster for any nicknames or shortened versions of long names. Better to know a person's preference than to shy away from conversation (and validation) because you are unsure.

For each student whose name you call, prompt him or her to answer a simple but random question. *What is your favorite snack food? What is the coolest thing you have ever found? What is the worst-smelling place you have ever been to?* Answers reveal a little something about the student's personality without getting too personal or intrusive. See the list in the appendix for more first-day questions.

Then it's your turn. Invite that same student to ask *you* a question. The whole rest of the school year is going to be about you asking students to do things that you would also do yourself because you believe in its merit: reading, writing, speaking, solving problems, and so forth. Put yourself out there and let students interview you on the first day. With the invitation to ask their teacher anything, students lean in and listen close—a key first step to working together.

Consider the alternative: Teachers go off on some boring tale about where they went to school and show pictures of their family and pets, subjecting a trapped audience to information they did not ask for. Instead, give students permission to ask you what they want to know and answer—appropriately—in return. Not only are students getting to know each other and you, but their voices are also in the room. If students do not speak on the first day, they have made no investment other than showing up and sitting. Your class culture, you have decided, will be better than that.

TRAINING THE SERVER

Teachers anticipate success, but does everyone have a plan for addressing failure? Think about how servers balance trays of food as they walk from the kitchen to the table. Their skill must come from lots of practice, prioritizing, and perhaps a few spills along the way. Drop a glass? Pick it up! Spill a whole dish? Start over with a smile. Well, how do teachers balance the expectations for success when the rest of life (family, friends, faith, fitness, and finances) also demands a share? You just don't know until it is all in your hands.

When you fail, model humility and ownership in the recovery. The transparency you show through reflection and action in moments of failure can instruct others just as well as moments of success. The work ethic students adopt comes from their environment. Let your words, thoughts, and actions make the learning community a positive and productive one. Bear in mind that stressed leaders replicate stressed followers.

Describe and model the difference between procedures and rules. Show students how to enter, how to exit, how to hand papers in, how to conduct a civil debate, and so on. Think like a server: Is it deliver on the left, pick up from the right . . . or is it the other way around? What do students say regarding classroom procedures that work best for them? Take the risk of asking students the best way to do things and your room will be the safe place it needs to be. The dictatorship model of classroom governance faded away decades ago. Students will love providing the suggestions and often will reveal an element to simplify the process that all the degreed adults in the building have not noticed or considered.

What is the walk-in procedure? Will students be asked to complete a bell-ringer task? Is the list of today's target and learning activities posted for students to preview? If it takes a few minutes to get class started after the bell, how much more preparation and narrowing could be preloaded into the transition time?

As important as the opener is to getting an engaging lesson started, it is the closure that can either seal in the goodness or cause the investment to disintegrate. One disturbing trend is allowing the final three minutes of the class period to become a time of decompression, shutdown, bag packing, and standing by the door. What should the procedure be instead? Forty-eight minutes of methodically planned instruction can unravel and unload at the door if students are simply standing, hands inching toward pocketed cell phones, waiting at the threshold for the bell to ring so they can escape.

In what ways could the opening and closing activities mirror each other, bringing the session full circle? What role can students play in this design? Why should the burden be on the teacher? Use a web-based name randomizer or select a student volunteer to be the one responsible for recapping the previous day's learning. Not only does this help connect today's activities to prior knowledge, but it also serves as a mutually owned accountability check. What a great way to reset session priorities from the recent hallway happenings and help those who were absent (or absentminded) without the concern of leaving someone behind.

The student of the day leads the review but can get support from classmates as needed. This is a team effort and not a quiz. If it takes three students to fill in all the details from yesterday's lesson and preview today's, so be it. Allow the first student to summarize the responses others contributed so the knowledge becomes owned and not borrowed. Mirror the same activity toward the end of the class session. What did we accomplish today? Are there any independent tasks due soon? What will we look forward to doing next?

Do students clearly understand classroom policies like homework and late work? Just as the in-class lessons need to have an anchored purpose, so do the take-home ones. Why should students invest the time to complete this task? Beyond points, what is the reward? What skills will this homework develop, and why must it be done independently? Is this being assigned to keep the student busy? Is it simply leftovers because time ran out? Intentional homework design must have a purpose if students are expected to complete it well. More on the topic of homework and late work appears in chapter 4.

This training of what students are expected to do and what choices they have must be clear to them from the very beginning. Alterations to this plan are natural and likely to occur, but massive or frequent overhauls could undermine your authority as a classroom manager. Be flexible when listening to customer concerns yet firm when pointing to clear standards. Yes, Angelica, you may bring a small stuffed animal if it helps you relax; no, you may not bring a live iguana.

THE DISCIPLINE PLAN

One quick way to damage or even completely destroy a safe classroom community is to call out a misbehaving student in front of everyone. Not much can communicate insensitivity more than making public someone else's faults. Effective and compassionate interventions are based on good rapport. Though rarely used in a smooth-running, student-centered environment, establish and make known the discipline intervention plan. Students can and should help with this.

As coauthors to much of what the year will involve, students know, in a general sense, what passes for acceptable and what defines inappropriate. For those times when self-control cannot curb a behavior, engage the multistep and mutually agreed upon system of awareness and correction, one that respects the individual and keeps the focus on learning. Draft this together as a class constitution of sorts. See figure 2.1 for an example.

A scaffolded approach ranging from a look to a local and discreet conversation to a short walk outside the room gives students multiple opportunities to de-escalate an attitude and a disruption before reaching the more serious consequences. If a staff member's first move is a referral to the principal's office, what opportunities does a student have to learn the correct adjustment in the moment? Maintaining the productivity of the learning environment remains everyone's priority. That way, any corrective action isn't just about the adult; it's about everyone.

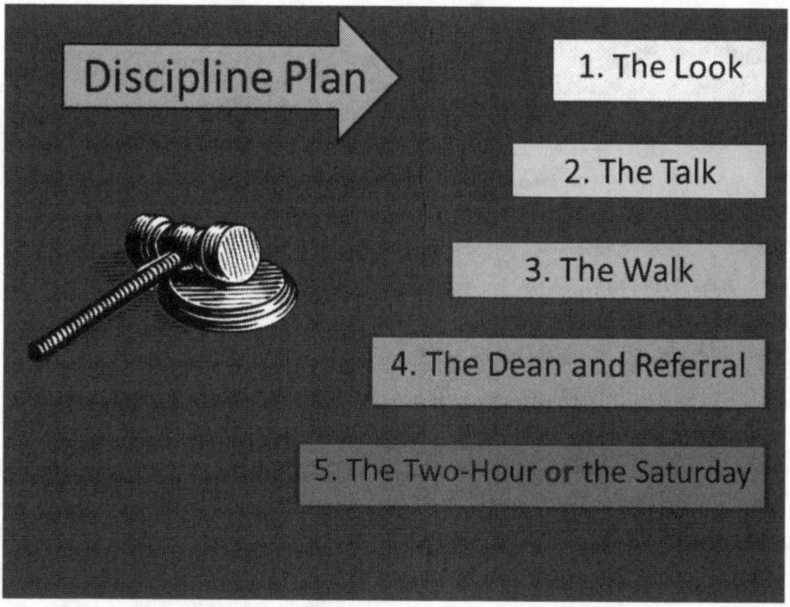

Figure 2.1. A discipline plan created with and for students. ***John M. Hayward***

A teacher determined to remain in control will often traverse from one stressful situation to the next. The misbehaving student, whose actions can unfairly be associated with his or her personality, will have no motivation for change. However, the teacher who holds each investor accountable for maintaining a productive climate and who encourages students to do the same for each other, will experience greater peace and results.

YOU NEVER TRULY KNOW UNTIL YOU ARE THERE

All the excitement and anticipation of the opening weeks of school will prepare you for only a fraction of what the reality brings. Who can predict the impact and influence of the differing personalities entering the classroom until you are standing there and soaking up the moment? Stress less, and let your school's vision, improvement plan, curriculum, and professional standards be your guide. Students will drive and decide much of the rest of what makes a school tick, and they should; the building and the services are for them anyway.

Even the best restaurants, with bold plans and alternative themes, have to acclimate to their clientele to safeguard their future. Think of how many drive-thru restaurants stay open late because owners realize that is when consumers are most likely to make purchases. The all-day breakfast idea did not come from management; it came from consumers, who influenced management to make the change.

Kelly Herkert reflects on the number of new, tantalizing sandwich creations patrons have created through the build-your-own feature on the menu. If a unique grilled cheese combination continues to be popular, it will earn a more permanent role. The rotation of options does not rely solely on the proprietor.

Have an ear that respectfully listens to suggestions and the humility to accept that perhaps someone else's idea will work more effectively than yours. In that instance, the objective did not change, only the path did. Stuck on finding a solution to something? Ask students! The answer you are looking for may be sitting right in front of you.

CHAPTER 2 FOOD FOR THOUGHT

What can you do from the first day onward to recognize the unique qualities of each student in your class?

How will you ensure your classroom is a safe and comfortable environment for all learners?

Why is it important to establish a relationship before instruction?

This fed my thinking:

I am hungry to pursue or try:

Chapter Three

How People See Things

Glass Half Full?

DO YOU NOTICE THE NEED?

Does it sometimes impress you when a member of the wait staff at a restaurant brings you exactly what you need before you ask? *How did they know I needed extra napkins or an ice water to complement my diet cola?* Attention to detail and the drive to quickly follow through ingrain in the server the ability to sense and deliver a patron's request. Educators can do the same for students beyond offering a pencil when someone rummages in a backpack at the start of a writing prompt. What deeper levels of awareness are possible in a student-centered environment?

ZOOMING IN

Teacher, make it your mission, your intention, to notice something new about as many students as possible each day. Think less of interrogation and more simply about observation. If a student is having a bad day, for example, you will know because his or her mannerisms will be different than the norm. If you have invested the time to record these changes, then you will be able to read depression, anxiety, fear, elation, and boredom in the faces of those who frequent your room. Incorporating gained insights from this emotional literacy can lead to quick alterations in lessons and ensure a productive session for everyone instead of creating disaster.

You do not have to compliment students on their appearance; this can become tiresome daily and lose its meaning or be just plain awkward. Implement a welcome procedure in the hallway or at the door where you intentionally make eye contact, read gait and expression, and engage in any conversation that students themselves initiate. The expression "they won't care what you know until they know that you care" takes on new life at the threshold of your room.

Being present and transparent builds trust and shows, without words, your truer passions. Students are done with teachers whose preclass passions include getting a fourth cup of coffee, checking e-mails, sports scores, or scrambling to finish lesson planning. Certainly, take care of personal business (How precious is getting to go to the bathroom?), but when you are just moments away from asking students for their undivided attention, it pays to offer some of your own.

When students enter the room, the best thing a teacher can do is exude anticipation for the awesomeness about to occur. A valued guest becomes a more willing participant. Why do restaurants and even some megastores have greeters? Managers know that a personal connection sets a positive tone for the rest of the patron's experience. The success of education, therefore, also relies on the power of relationships.

As customers enter Everdine's restaurant in Naperville, they hear a staff member deliver a cheery welcome either from the counter or the kitchen. Service and attention begins upon entering. Want your students to get cartloads of goodness out of your class or try something new from *your* menu? Observe and respond to those directly in front of you.

Here's a crazy thought: What if a student of the day joined you as a cogreeter at the door? What levels of empathy and understanding would develop within your school community? The animosity a student may harbor for another individual or even a group could have a chance to melt away under the circumstances of seeing them differently. Certainly, preteens and teenagers are people watchers, but under most circumstances, it is for the sake of comparison. Change that for the genuine compassion of a greeting and a new level of understanding begins.

Here is another possibility: What if on the days of exams, students entering the building walked through an encouraging pep line? Available teacher and staff volunteers could hold signs that say "You got this!" or other motivational coaching quotes and offer high fives for the weary and worried. Would test scores improve if morale got a boost at the door? Try this encouraging relationship-starter and see!

STAYING IN THE ZONE

During the lesson, stay in the zone of an observer. Now that you have established what kind of day everyone is having, you can move on to gauging how everyone is digesting the learning opportunities. In a student-centered classroom, the teacher has more freedom to observe and facilitate a lesson while students take a more active role in the activity's implementation, direction, and follow-through.

Here is a likely scenario: Laura is reading aloud and everyone except Oscar is following along. The teacher moves closer to the area where Oscar is sitting and makes observations from several angles about why this might be so. *Why did he not notice that everyone else turned the page of the book?* No one else freaks out or loses focus as the teacher slowly leans over the text in Oscar's hands and points to the paragraph Laura just started. If Oscar adjusts, the teacher zooms back out to the class as a whole and resumes watching and participating. If the redirection fails, the teacher stays in the moment and tries another tool—all without words—to value the student and the precious seconds away from the task.

Performing the above actions proves several things. Lesson flow matters. What you accomplish here today happens for a valuable purpose. If students created the lesson, you demonstrate a respect for their efforts and share a hope for good results. Oscar matters. In your room, students and their diverse needs will not be overlooked. The demands of the agenda will never overshadow the needs of a learner. Literacy matters. Everyone in the building encourages literacy growth, and the unique methods you use each day are aimed at helping students improve in the way you know each learns best. Community matters, because the teacher is not alone in knowing and showing that people come first.

Eventually, the students in a well-centered and value-focused classroom will conduct their own peer-to-peer interventions. Someday, the student next to Oscar will lean over and redirect without the teacher having to intervene because the task itself is so engaging and promises reward. Maybe the investors themselves have played a part in the lesson design, so they will retain the role of enforcers to see that the lesson proceeds as planned.

How different this will be from the uncomfortably frequent scenario where students challenge and resist instruction in attempts to derail the teacher's perfect lesson! When students share in activity creation and community building, they commit themselves to seeing the plan succeed.

SEEING BEYOND

What happens in class today influences and informs what happens this week, which, in turn, helps students prepare for unit-long and course objectives. Help students see where, how, and why this particular stretch of minutes fits into the overall plan. Say it aloud before the "Why are we doing this?" question surfaces. Anticipate that someone will want to know the purpose of today's activities and address it before giving the directions. How will engagement in this particular task benefit individual student goals and make use of (and challenge) current levels of understanding? What students really want to know is, *Am I doing this because the skill will be tested or is there more lifelong value to this?*

Be clear about purpose with statements like these:

- "This feedback form will provide direction to how we interpret and conduct tomorrow's writing workshop."
- "The film clip we are about to watch will confirm for some of you the emotional tension you sensed when we read the passage. For those who feel differently, this will establish a great starting point for tomorrow's conversation."
- "Your research for the next few minutes on the website Amanda recommended for us will yield sources that will complement or contradict the claim you are trying to prove. Both are valuable, and in the discussion that follows, we will discover why."

Activities, learning opportunities, and even assessments each point to something ahead, or at least they should. Communicate this clearly and often so students will not want or need to ask "What's the point?" Everyone should be able to verbalize the purpose for a task; those who cannot will only conclude that they are doing busywork.

Dare to invite a response as a test of student awareness. "Can three students, any three, each identify one way this reading and the activity that follows will help us achieve the learning standards for this unit?" What if no one answers? Is it possible the motivation or the aim of the activity does *not* have a curricular value? Time to adjust!

What gain is there for a student who completes a task without knowing its purpose? Many times, students only ask how many points something is worth and disregard the reason for doing the task. Remember, compliance is not part of the curriculum nor does it pass for engaged learning; completion does not always reflect comprehension. Help students see beyond today and make connections to long-term and better-retained learning.

ADJUST THE RAMP

An advertisement for a moving company illustrates their significant selling point: a lower loading ramp than the competition. This, the ad says, will make the goal of loading the truck and moving forward much easier to achieve.

A reasonable goal or expected standard of loading the moving truck and relocating possessions is to get said items safely and securely on board. So if the loading ramp needs to be lower to achieve this desired end, why would it matter to other workers involved in the moving process? Does a national norm for ramp height exist, or is a fully and safely loaded truck the desired outcome? Clearly, individuals may use the ramp of their choosing, but if a higher ramp makes the task of loading the truck impossible, disheartening, or even hazardous, shouldn't one have the option to change it?

The literacy practices in classrooms are, in a sense, an opportunity to load students with strategies, insights, and perspectives on the world around them—first as consumers and then as producers. Each day, educators encourage readers to embrace and own the materials in front of them and add skills to their ever-growing collection of resources. At the end of the school year, schools (and/or states) assess a student's acquisition of these skills, and it is a full truck that matters, isn't it? The final score comparison is all about what is in the truck, not about what method(s) was used to get it in there.

If the ramp is too high, students will not successfully retain those skills, secure them in long-term memory, or be able to move those skills forward.

With this understanding, you can now see why a D student in September is often still a D student in May or why a fifth-grade reading level does not change in three consecutive semesters: No one adjusted the ramp.

Getting students on board with learning is a challenge. A teacher's professional mission, however, is not to continue pushing the same challenging plan until the student either makes it or gives up. A teacher's passion is to find a way—even after introducing various methods—to meet the student at the level of accessibility and transfer confidence and skills across the threshold into permanent storage.

A MATTER OF PERSPECTIVE

The way one person sees things is not how everyone else does or should. Students come to school with experiences seemingly generalized or stereotyped yet incredibly diverse. The home lives of today's students, whether you learn this through short conversations with them or from indirect reports, include elements not experienced in any previous generation. Your childhood and upbringing, however recent, is not the same as that of your students. What you value as a positive, today's kids may not.

Even after all the movies and television shows portraying family dysfunction, something new and horrible will arise that you have not even considered. Therefore, teachers have no idea what contributes to how a student may view just one line of a poem, a sentence of a text, or a math problem. How a student reacts to a photo, a film clip, a piece of writing, or even a comment in class does not come from a place disconnected from prior experience. Who wants to try solving problem number three when solving what to eat today is a bigger concern?

In a safe, student-centered environment, students can freely share emotions and perspectives without fear of judgment. In these transparent conversations, walls of prejudice break down, and students see each other and their valuable differences in a new light. This community is one where being open and vocal is encouraged because the resulting perspective is one people need in order to build empathy and eliminate prejudice. Listening is as valuable a skill as speaking, and anyone can model how to do so respectfully.

The inflexible classroom dominated by an agenda, strict timetable, or dictator-like rigidity that does not allow student voice will never get to experience such a level of depth or growth. What new insights will students gain in a class where their own risk taking controls the flow of instruction? Keep the standards at the forefront, yet let the students make the choices. The dangers of limiting students to one way of thinking are clear.

MULTIPLE VIEWS IN ONE ROOM

So how does this flexibility impact the classroom? First, please recognize that the interpretations students offer when they explain things come from lenses that are not "wrong." Some people buy their sunglasses from high-end outlets, some from huts. Lenses alter our view, but unless we have put on pitch-black blinders, we simply see things differently. Second, these diverse perspectives reflect the real world our students long to, and soon will, experience.

Open conversations enrich culture and enliven classrooms. Let them happen. Guide students through the process of gathering evidence from the text to support their argument. If a student sees something meaningful in the painting that you did not consider, that does not make it wrong. If the student solved the problem or conducted the experiment using a method you had not anticipated but arrived at the answer, why should the student be made to feel wrong? Often, for the instructor, this is where the greatest and most barrier-breaking and lasting learning takes place. "Oh," someone will say, "I had not thought about it that way before."

Some things remain facts and do not have a perspective. One cannot argue against the fact that *Star Wars: Episode IV* came out in 1977.

For some contexts, there *is* a discernable wrong perspective. A love story, for example, has an obvious wrong territory if someone tries to argue the author wants to bring attention to the plight of undernourished penguins in Antarctica. Someone can still be *that* wrong.

Customer service is hard work. Sometimes the wait staff will have to lean in closer or ask a patron to repeat something slowly. This is all in an effort to get the order just right and bring the client satisfaction and enjoyment. The kitchen crew at Everdine's remakes sandwiches any time someone requests it. Your local baristas remake specialty coffee orders every day. Managers are watching to make sure this quality control happens on a regular basis so customers will return and bring their friends. As a classroom manager, your responsibility and motivation is the same.

CHAPTER 3 FOOD FOR THOUGHT

What needs to change in your everyday practice that will enable you, safely and appropriately, to know students individually?

How can student input (voice) play a larger role in your class?

Why is it beneficial for students to be exposed to multiple perspectives on the issues discussed in class?

This fed my thinking:

I am hungry to pursue or try:

Chapter Four

When Customers Ask for More

BE TRANSPARENT ABOUT YOUR OWN STRUGGLES

You are an expert in your content area—especially when you are open with students about how you overcame *your* initial struggles as a student engaging with and understanding that content. Were you born reading chemistry labs? You sketched quadratic equations in the preschool sandbox? No, somewhere in your academic pursuits, you narrowed your interest to a specific discipline.

For example, how did you, as a college student, discover the best ways to decipher and remember the course content and companion texts? To you, your content area is like your favorite restaurant. You have been here so many times that you have no trouble with the menu or the atmosphere. Walk right in, sit right down; you are comfortable here. Your students, however, have never been here and find navigating the environment a little intimidating.

Meet each student at this point, right at the threshold between comfortable and terrifying. What worked for you? If a student responds to the advice you model and adopts this method for themselves, great. Not everyone will, but this is a great place to start.

To reach students who do not adopt your method of engagement with the material and concepts, rotate through various approaches that are equally engaging and accessible. Your goal is to get each student into a learning style and text-unlocking method that works. Yes, in a class of twenty-eight students, you may have to work tirelessly to identify as many inroads as possible, but isn't that the goal?

On the back wall at Everdine's, the Herkerts hung a large chalkboard to display their menu. In large, well-written, colorful letters, patrons can easily read the choices. Because Brian and Kelly expect there to be changes, revision is as easy as erase and rewrite. If a potential customer lingers too long in indecision, Kelly or Christine, a cashier and line-prep specialist, will approach to clarify the possibilities. Walking into the restaurant indicates a hunger. A personal, interested intervention from staff brings that customer closer to his or her desired outcome.

Differentiation, whether you realize it or not, is how you gravitated toward the successful methods you eventually adopted. Students are not at eventually yet; they are still at search, discover, try, fail, recover. Coach students through your journey of academic development and show them how effective various learning strategies can be. The goal of education is not to make students replicate the one way you learn; it is to encourage students to discover and adopt the way *they* each learn best.

At the beginning of the school year, and carrying through as often as necessary, be a transparent reader and learner in front of students. Think aloud when pausing in the middle of a sentence. Make mistakes in pronunciation, not to mock those who struggle, but to model how to recover. Use context clues or look up words instead of just assuming you know their meaning so students discover this as a valuable and rewarding practice. Get stuck solving an equation and narrate the steps in reverse to identify new paths. Test the hypothesis aloud. Engage in the wonder of history or art as if you are seeing it for the first time, not simply rehashing what you have known for years. Question often, and explain everything. Assume nothing is a given and once again students will catch on to the joy of discovery they hopefully had in their early elementary days.

Then let go of the lead. What seems terrifying for you is actually the exciting empty space of possibility where students fill in the blanks instead. Say, "That's the extent of what I know today. Let's hear at least three new insights from you on this." Sit down and wait through the awkward silence as brains all around you stretch, fill, leap, grasp, and share what you just ushered them into creating. What beautiful things happen next is called authentic learning.

THE SILENT TREATMENT

Speaking of awkward silences, classes whose culture is noncommittal to conversation can still become lively idea-sharing forums. You want to propose a topic and watch students run with it; the topic, like an inflated beach ball, bouncing from one participant to the next, but this isn't happening in your room and it frustrates you. Or only a handful of students dominate the airtime. Students just need a little encouragement!

The saying "Penny for your thoughts" invites an all-in game for hearing every voice in the room. From a metal tin or plastic bowl, give students two pennies each. Set up the container with the remaining coins on a stool or desk in the center of the room. Regardless of the topic or question prompt, each student must chip one penny into the container before speaking. Each person must contribute but can only have two turns. The fun of attempting to toss the coin into the bin from their seat softens the tension in the room, and then students turn to attend to the speaker. After conducting this activity just a few times, students will realize their input matters and that multiple viewpoints strengthen the discussion.

Another activity to help students connect their thoughts with others and to extend conversations for several minutes requires the use of thread. Give each student a five-inch length of twine or thin yarn. For each comment someone makes, encourage them to literally connect to the previous speaker's words. Encourage signal phrases like "I agree with Mark when he says . . ." or "While Tess is right about that, I also believe . . ." When finished speaking, the student knots his or her thread to the end of the previous speaker's length and waits to see if someone speaks next.

Post these completed discussion threads in the room for a day so students can see the value of extending and connecting thoughts in engaging discussions. Have contests to determine how long a topic can last. Eight speakers in a row? Fourteen? Teachers often want to open and close conversations themselves, but what if students take ownership of the entire process? Their voices are so valuable to everyone's growth. Brainstorm additional ways to make contributing to class irresistible and add these methods to your toolbox.

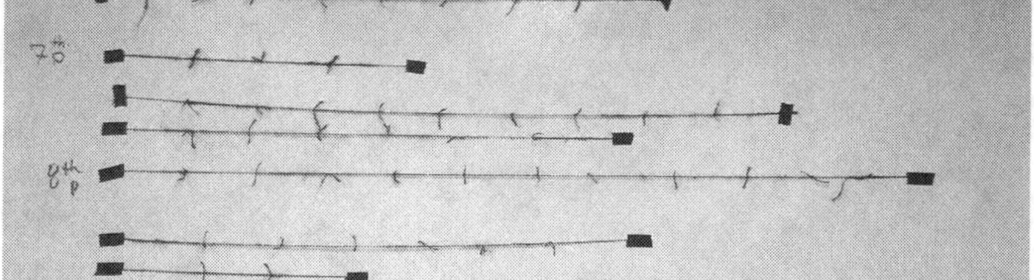

Figure 4.1. See which class can string together the longest discussion. ***John M. Hayward***

LIVE IN THEIR WORLD FOR A MOMENT

Write when students write. Solve when they solve. Providing a learning opportunity in the form of a prompt to keep students occupied may be a tempting opening so you can fill the time with self-serving tasks. Checking e-mail, planning the next lesson, even grading may appear to be worthwhile, on-task activities while students are working, but the more teachers distance themselves from the student experience, the harder it is to effectively coach, intervene, empathize, and change.

When students tackle an in-class writing task, join them. Set up your own lab station in chemistry and work alongside, not above, the path to discovery. Solve an equation the same way students do. Be transparent about your own discoveries and thinking. Share your insights aloud and encourage others to do the same.

If you encounter challenges and breakthroughs, imagine what students face. If you get bored making your way through an outline, for example, guess what? Discuss the process of learning having lived it in the moment. Reflection helps teachers learn. Students are more likely to engage when they see their teachers taking the same risk. Empathy grows when teachers occupy the same trenches as students, battling and recovering through challenges together.

Instead of assuming students know how to conduct sound research, model every research method imaginable. Tired of students conducting Google-only searches? Then stop doing the same thing in front of them. Try something new each time you need to find information. What worked? What will you try next? Lead the path to discovery or be teachable yourself and let others share their expertise. Do not complain about students not getting it right if you make the same mistakes yourself.

An educator's goal is to bring everyone to new understanding, not necessarily to lead them every time. If a student shows you how to do something (like that's never happened with audiovisual equipment), do not feel humiliated; celebrate learning as an opportunity and an advantage. It is perfectly acceptable to yield to a student's expertise and surrender your dry-erase marker or laptop and display screen for a student-turned-instructor in the room to complete the moment.

What strategies will your room full of instructors deliver next? Problem solve as a community with emphasis on the valuable contributions of each individual. Have you ever been to an escape-room experience or played a Breakout EDU game? All participants gets an opportunity to bring their genius to the table and in the process realizes their slice of intelligence is not all that is necessary to solve a problem.

The progress needed to make it through the curriculum will come to nothing if people are left behind wondering how to get back up on their feet.

As much as students are likely to think teachers live in underground laboratories constructing evil plots in the form of quizzes or packets, educators and administrators can do much to avoid making this image manifest. Without a foundation of securing students' knowledge of how to stumble, how to fail, and how to seek out assistance, whatever gets built afterward will mean little.

Playing dumb is not what this is; call it transparency. Be real and students will attend. If it worked for you, then you are the most eligible spokesperson. By the end of the year, will students in your class have become their own spokesperson, testifying to others about how they have improved . . . or will students complain about how they did not get your one way of doing things and immediately look forward to having a different teacher next semester?

AVOID BEING OF FIXED MIND-SET YOURSELF ABOUT STRATEGIES

Learners who harbor the fixed mind-set that every task will be an impossible challenge have little to look forward to throughout the year. Readers who believe they will never understand the text preload their thinking with failure every time the skill arises. Writers who have no strategies to combat blocked thoughts will wince every time a prompt is introduced. Coming to the board to solve a math problem is torture for a student who already believes that he or she will only embarrass him- or herself. If a student is convinced speaking in front of an audience will always be difficult, what could improve that student's confidence? Possessing a fixed mind-set as a teacher does nothing to improve the cycle of mediocrity that many students identify with year after year.

Even if the rumor about incoming students pegs them as a "difficult" class, giving them a chance to establish their identities anew may be the most valuable and exclusive opportunity they have to prove the negative image wrong.

THERE IS MORE THAN ONE WAY TO LEARN

Did you know there is more than one way to eat spaghetti? Maybe you are a scooper and someone else is a twirler. Either way, the food ultimately gets consumed. Do you eat sandwiches from the top crust down, in from the side, or without crusts at all and bite as you rotate the sandwich like a turntable? Have you met a person who eats the tip off the bottom of an ice cream cone first and then eats from the top down before it melts? If this image threatens your comfort, you know the feeling of fixed thinking.

Even the planning of instruction and assessments can fall victim to fixed thinking. Remember that while one destination remains set at the end of the semester, multiple paths are available for getting there. Multiple routes, one destination. What new avenues will students help you find for the achievement of these goals? Instead of one viewpoint, incorporate the investors in the process and yield to the most effective, promising, and rewarding ideas when they arise.

Communicate with colleagues for brainstorming before proceeding with a new lesson plan. Get feedback from informal observers and conduct some observations of your own. The theory of multiple intelligences becomes valid when you can see it in action, and in a building of so many talented teachers and students, you are bound to see it if you look hard enough. The way to solve the issue that has eluded you so far has already been solved in someone else's classroom or experience. Do the human research and remain deferential enough to alter your own perspective. You will become a better teacher, and your students will become better learners in the process.

AGE EQUALS ATTENTION SPAN

A seven-year-old second grader can be expected to attend to a single-moded task for about seven minutes. A high school sophomore, about fifteen minutes. Pushing this demand beyond the time limit will require either higher engagement, higher reward, or lots of disciplined training of skills. Threats and reprimands do nothing to enhance a child's ability to sustain attention to an activity, so freshen it up.

If you have a student struggling to overcome ADD (attention deficit disorder) or ADHD (attention deficit hyperactivity disorder), conduct class in a way that includes movement, flexibility, or at least a rut-busting mode change every few minutes. Exhausting? Not when compared to the frustration of policing off-task behavior in an endurathon of activity for students who cannot help it. And isn't that the real issue? Too many teachers believe the attention-deficit student can help him- or herself or snap out of it because the activity structure itself (or the corresponding commands) should be engaging enough to curb the tendency to wander. Nope. For success with this population, plan activities in an age-equals-attention-span approach and enjoy the successes students can experience when the format accommodates their style, not the teacher's style.

WIN THE BAROMETER

The thermostat in a classroom is a sensitive device often labeled with a "hands off" sign written in faded ink on an index card from years earlier. Someone had the foresight, or the disgust, to post this notice as a warning not to mess with the comfort level. "Don't touch that dial!" Finding that delicate balance of warmth and humidity requires several measurements and adjustments, and no one wants to have to go through that all over again. Identifying and maintaining the *emotional* balance of the classroom may be more difficult.

Then into this environment comes the outlier, the student whose behavior draws much more attention and respect, humor, and energy from the class than the teacher can tolerate. The climate-changer seeks to upset the teacher's world in favor of his or her own and often derails carefully planned instruction. You thought the teacher was the only one in control? *This* child is the barometer.

Ha! You thought the climate of the class was controlled from the front, where the teacher sits, didn't you? Many times, the second set of controls, with an opposing set of motives, sits in the back. Winning this child becomes a teacher's strategic priority, and the sooner the better. Instead of making enemies and oppositions, make alliances and seek understanding.

The root cause of the desire to disrupt often has nothing to do with the teacher's personality; it is the teacher's insistence to be in control and the inability to see the child's truer issues that cause conflict. Do not let go of everything (that is surrender and loss); let go of some as a bargain for partnership. To achieve the "everybody wins" classroom, each student needs to feel a sense of ownership—*especially* those who look to the barometer instead of the teacher for direction.

You know the scenario. The teacher introduces an activity, something new, something involving risk. Instead of looking attentively at the teacher for instructions and guidance, students around the room are sneaking glances at the barometer to see if engagement will be worth it. See how it works now? Win the barometer, win the remnant of the class not with you initially.

See the person behind the mask of disruptive behavior. What is the student's motive for wanting to be funny, in control, or desired? Getting to know this element of the individual is the secret to maintaining a comfortable balance of instruction, learning, and opportunity for all. Once the thermostat of classroom climate is set, you should not have to touch it again for the rest of the year. You don't have to touch students physically in order to make a connection; you do, however, have to reach their hearts and hear their stories.

THERE IS MORE THAN ONE WAY TO TEACH

Consider how even a chef whose fame may ride on a signature dish must also battle to keep a diverse audience of patrons satisfied. Diners will tire of macaroni and cheese if that is all you know. Sure, there is simplicity in sameness, but there is also the likelihood of specializing yourself out of a career. Have more than one teaching style; your instructional toolbox should look more diverse than Charlie Brown's clothes closet.

In order to reach students whose strengths in learning models vary, the instructor needs to know how to diversify the delivery. Breaking out of one's favorite sweet spot is the hardest part. Personality may center a teacher on one mode of instruction. For example, lecturers love to speak and dominate the conversation, leaving little time for student interaction and development. Hands-off teachers let the materials do the teaching. (Remember Ditto from the movie *Teachers*?)

Why do restaurant menus have scores of options for their patrons? So they will enjoy the experience and come back for more. Okay, so you are at a reception dinner and get handed a plate with ingredients you didn't customize. You can handle that for *one* day. But before 175 days have passed, you will have pined for change. Do not be a one-dish menu for customers you see five days a week.

Learners tire of sameness. Isn't this what professional development workshops offer a break from? Embrace opportunities to observe and expand.

Kelly Herkert shares the secret of keeping up with the latest in the restaurant business: spy missions and seminars. "I don't bring a physical notebook with me to other restaurants, but believe me, I am taking notes," she says. Since you have already determined it is best to remain teachable, be ready to have more than one tool in your instructional kit.

STRATEGIES FOR STUDENT-CENTERED LEARNING: A SAMPLER PLATTER

The following strategies aim to break the routine of teacher-led instruction through opportunities for students to make some choices for themselves. If these sound like things you already do, then you are on your way to an engaging, student-centered model of teaching. If these strategies make you uncomfortable because of their nontraditional format, consider them as a suggestion from a teacher who has been there too and has made a welcome change.

Chef, the following recipes for success may help your learners who long for a personalized dish of methodology finally experience and adopt lasting habits.

Your classroom is not entirely like a restaurant, yet in some ways your instructional delivery, methods, and atmosphere can serve and satisfy the individual tastes of students. The fun challenge is helping students identify what they have a taste for, which will differ greatly from person to person. A customized approach grows out of observing, surveying, and listening to the needs around you.

If one student prefers to digest the material you have prepared while sitting on the floor, why discourage the practice? In a classroom where students have opportunities to discover and develop their individual learning styles, success follows. Identifying how students read, write, study, and speak best may be as simple as rotating enough examples and exposures in the planning menu to let these learning palates develop.

The "safe risk" of personalized task setting means you have one destination but many possible methods of arrival. Set the mission before students by clarifying specifically what the objective is and why, but resist limiting the options to one mode of travel. Remember that lesson planning is like sending a reconnaissance plane out to gather intelligence. Without a specific mission, the plane will simply hover over and circle the target, not landing on anything, and will return to base with little to no results.

Sure, you may offer, "Class, this is one way I recommend reaching the standard," but consider how you can include, "What are some other ways you see of getting there?" Customization begins with choice, gets refined through observation, and confirms its usefulness through increased skill retention, academic enjoyment (not an oxymoron), and ultimately the student's performance.

"READ HOW YOU READ BEST": A BUFFET OF OPTIONS

Reading happens in every class, not just language arts. Employing literacy skills to unlock meaning occurs continuously throughout a student's school day. Remaining attentive to students' needs means getting to know them as readers.

What if instead of shepherding students through every possible reading-intervention idea and research-based strategy, teachers take note of what students *themselves* would choose? Perhaps teachers can identify the challenges and weaknesses of readers through observation instead of testing. The option of reading a chapter of the text in the pose and method students themselves feel to be most effective could indicate the difference between those who know what works and those who have not yet arrived at an effective method.

If you think about it, modeling a rotation of study methods works the same way: Introduce five different ways students may adopt new vocabulary, and let them individually gravitate toward the one that resonates with their own retention and comfort. One size *does not* fit all. Does the same approach apply to other instructional strategies? This perspective and practice of creating an environment where students are exposed to variety is one step closer to getting personalization right.

Students are usually good sports about trying something new if it means getting them into an extended text or making any process easier. Starting a new unit with a book longer than two hundred pages? One day, play the audio book while students listen. Grant students the privilege of interrupting the flow at any time to contribute a "live annotation" in the moment of discovery or inquiry. If necessary, stop to explore what has intrigued or troubled the student and proceed when ready. Students can point out their insights and questions to each other as seen in figure 4.2. Plowing through the text toward completion is not the goal; understanding it first is.

Another day of the week, read the text aloud using different voices for different speakers in the text as needed. Sparing your voice, on a third day, have students read in a format called "Three Ring Circus." One group with you, one group with a volunteer or strong reader, and a third group of independent readers. While this is, in a way, personalized learning, students do not always seek out the support of teacher-guided reading when they clearly need it. So experiment with one additional scenario.

"Read How You Read Best" becomes an invitation for students to create the pose and environment where they believe their best reading and engagement with the text will occur. "Can we use our headphones?" Absolutely.

Figure 4.2. Students teaching students significant parts of the text. ***John M. Hayward***

"May I lay under the front table and make a reading cave for myself?" Sure, go ahead. Within the boundaries of the room, give students the freedom to prop backpacks like pillows, lean against walls, alcove themselves in the windowsills, and so on. Some may even choose to partner read quietly in an anyone-can-come corner of their own.

To some teachers, this freedom feels like a horrible compromise of standards and may even bristle those dedicated to more die-hard classroom management principles. This only proves the point, however, that students who are invited to discover their best method for learning often find it sooner and adopt full implementation.

Students who read how they read best are actually reading. If a student with a 60 percent in October still has a 60 percent grade point average for reading comprehension in May, what benefit has there been to thirty weeks of planning and instruction? Both flexibility and frustration can lead teachers to new approaches, but the former is much more enjoyable than the latter.

Personalized learning allows students to experience the acquisition of skills and demonstrate the mastery of skills in formats customized to and acknowledging their diverse styles. Stand back and watch in nervous anticipation: What will students do with the time and method of their own choosing? Each student will likely self-govern his or her own attention to task and adjust to avoid distractions as needed.

Those who struggle with independence will do so in such an obvious way that the teacher's intervention to redirect back to task can be immediate. Engagement will remain so high and undisturbed that you may often have to let learning moments linger beyond the time planned. While this activity may not occur on a daily basis, students will show improvement and remain committed to making the most of this time when it comes up again in the future.

Reading builds empathy for other people and their varying emotional states, helps students access language for understanding their world and communicating it back to different audiences, and, according to recent research, could even assist people to have more positive, productive, and longer lives. Keep reading a priority in your class and model good reading yourself whenever possible. Be vocal and transparent about your reading interests while inviting the same from your students. A community developed around a safe embrace of accessible literacy strategies and resources grows and strengthens in observable, meaningful, and memorable ways.

Would students reach the same level of self-awareness if they could explore a math problem, write a journal prompt, and arrive at conclusions in the same manner? What could you learn about your students in this more natural environment of multimodal access to text? There is more than one way to engage even the most reluctant readers, and those students deserve the chance to try repeatedly.

A WORD ABOUT WRITING

Composition, like reading, is a disciplined practice with the expectation of producing something. Instead of decoding and arriving at new understanding, a writer creates this world for readers through word craft and structure. Similarly, just as students enter your class at varying levels of reading readiness, students' writing skills may be all over the map. Their previous instructors, the amount of exposure and support they received, and frankly, the feedback that has either shepherded them forward or stalled them in complacency are all factors in determining their readiness to write.

Be honest as you revisit your own comfort level with writing. What support can you give students on a prompt if you could not confidently complete the same? How would you even begin to assess something you could not master? If you feel the need for a skill refresher, be open to the opportunity, knowing there are only benefits to investing in the improvement of your composition skills. Take a class, study a professional resource manual, or work your way through a college composition textbook. When you share the writing-improvement journey with students, everyone grows in confidence and skill.

Listening to and observing your students throughout the writing process yields several benefits regardless of the content area. You will know where students struggle, what breakthroughs to celebrate, and why an extension to a due date might be worth offering.

Instructional methods need to vary here as well. Writers need a supportive environment, honest and timely feedback, the flexibility to revise, and clear expectations for purpose and audience. The process of writing as an organic, raw journey of discovery allows participants to risk finding and developing their voice. Facilitate this culture with the assistance of students whose comfort with writing can be a help to others. The goal is not simply to see where everyone is skill-wise and reflect a score; it is to move each student closer to self-realization and confidence through many trials and triumphs and, yes, potentially many drafts.

An effective writer's workshop means there is no master chef. Sure, there are clear expectations of quality, and, certainly, there are established non-negotiable conventions for the structure holding all the thoughts together, but each writer gets to create his or her own dish. Writing is not "wrong" per se, though there are varying degrees of clarity; writing is an art of expression. Each person is on a level field, wrestling with an idea and communicating it in a personalized way that an audience can understand.

Look at samples of varying quality. Read drafts aloud and anonymously to savor the texture of words together. Respect the time students will need to get the process started and support them through the challenges of checkpoints and deadlines. Embrace revision as a writer's reality. What famous work of art was completed and displayed to the public in its first draft?

This is also why requiring a certain word count or page length stifles artistic expression. Hold to expectations of quality in a range of expected paragraphs but not pages or words. A poorly sung melody does not improve with an extra chorus, a poorly acted movie does not improve with extended scenes, and a poorly written novel does not improve with an extra chapter. A student's skill at writing will show itself within the freedom to compose until the expression is complete. Any word-craft expectations beyond this threshold will be whipped up marshmallow fluff and contain little passion or truth.

You may have done it yourself in your academic past. A teacher expected a five-page essay and you were done in three and a half. So you played with the margins, increased the font, and extended sentences into diluted, unpalatable thoughts until they leaked onto the canvas of that fifth page. This is not authentic writing anymore. To the artist, it is insulting.

Listen to your students telling you they prefer to write freely and arrive at the ideal length for that message rather than having the parameters so prescribed. If we expect our students to compose beautiful symphonies, why do we dictate in advance how many notes it should take?

Think in paragraphs; teach paragraphs and model how to boxcar those separate units into an essay until the train is full to the writer's specifications. The skill being assessed will still be present, developing, or absent without having to prescribe specific lengths. Some teachers prefer to count words; others know it is better to make the words count.

STUDENT-CENTERED LESSON CREATION

One awesome way to know your lessons are reaching your target audience is to have the audience create and even conduct the lessons themselves. This is a risk, but a safe one that students, parents, and administrators support. The benefits are numerous, and all it takes is letting go a little.

Creating engaging lessons has always been one of your favorite elements of this profession, yet as you look ahead at a long string of weeks without a holiday, you sense something in the routine needs to give. Before students have a chance to register their teacher's fatigue or even consider complaining themselves, resolve to change the approach by letting go: Turn over the planning of lessons to students.

This makes sense, actually. Students should already participate in the grading process as coevaluators and rubric writers. They make noticeable sacrifices to maintain the strong community in your room. In what ways could they take the opportunity to plan their own learning activities and turn them into something more relevant, engaging, and differentiated?

Carve a new station into your rotation day and invite three random student volunteers to join you in the front of the room for a planning session. Ask them to bring only a notebook and their open minds; contribute a template for the daily target, the "Depth of Knowledge" wheel of engagement verbs, the unit standards, and whatever content folders the students may want to consult.

The mission is simple yet wide open: Plan this Friday's activities. Tell students that you can do the facilitating if they are not comfortable doing so (or you can team up), but the fifty minutes of instructional time is entirely theirs to construct. After an initial hesitation, somewhere along the lines of disbelief and awe (as if you had handed them the keys and said, "You drive"), they will map out some impressive age-appropriate, challenging, and varied activities that will meet every learning goal you hope to achieve.

The results may surprise you! Your college degree, extra planning period, even all the awesome professional development you have attended will not have ever come up with the lessons your students create for themselves. The rigor, the fun, the focus on accountability one would hope for should be present without much coaching or prompting. Okay, so you may have to remind groups that "Heads Up 7-Up" is not technically a valid formative assessment, but overall this risk will prove its worth and save all concerned from the doldrums. One activity students will *not* create for themselves, which should be a warning to teachers who rely on them, is filling out a packet. Given the opportunity, students have no desire to complete packets, even if self-constructed.

Expect to hear, "So this is what it's like for you." Maybe walking in your shoes will make them better-behaved students, but more important, they will become more aware of the *value* of their learning. Break down the us/them walls and work together at mapping the best path toward achieving unit and course objectives. Open your plan book; it's okay to be transparent.

COTEACHING WITH YOURSELF

Have you ever wanted to partner with another teacher and conduct a "stations" activity for your students? What if you could address a half or even a third of your class on occasion and give only that group very specific feedback or instructions? If you do not have a colleague or an aide with whom to share your instruction, remember that with recorded technology, you do. You can partner with yourself.

One concept of the "flipped" classroom model is to give students instruction at home and more hands-on practice and guidance in the classroom. Practice and application spread out to the most opportune parts of the day: independence outside of the classroom, when students can demonstrate levels of mastery with moderate challenge, and inside class, when support with the instructor is necessary. The preparation time you invest to create an extension of your classroom "for home" can also have beneficial uses for splitting your class while you are all assembled.

A split class or stations model allows a portion of the class to receive direct instruction from materials you have recorded or prepared, freeing you up to interact with the other portion of the class in person. Can you see how this would keep you available on a lab day in science?

Don't want to consume class time with a lecture? Prerecord it and set aside a section of the room for addressing this task while you engage learners in another task. Then rotate, reflect, respond. Not only is movement helpful for student retention of information but so is a diversified task list and more personal interaction from the instructor. Let the video, podcast, or back-channeled feedback do some of the teaching and data gathering while you address the smaller group of learners who need more individualized attention, and suddenly you are coteaching with yourself.

Even better is the classroom model where after a few sessions of you dividing the instruction, students take ownership of the teaching partner role and mentor themselves. What if your coteacher was a student who led a small group or a panel who taught a prepared body of material?

The classroom is still yours to plan and assess, but the coteaching elements of sharing the instructional load may already be at hand. Build trust through experimentation, and someday your students will be self-directed learners and evaluators too.

Coteaching can occur with:

1. A cocurricular colleague
2. A special education instructor or aide
3. A cross-curricular colleague or administrator
4. A guest
5. Web tools or prerecorded instruction
6. Students themselves

MORE THAN ONE WAY TO PROVIDE FEEDBACK

Providing timely and accurate personalized feedback gives students the support and encouragement they need to continue developing their academic and social-emotional skills. The guidance you and peers provide will steer students closer toward mastery in the criteria you, your school, and state and national standards provide. Without this feedback, students spacewalk in a vacuum of clarity regarding their level of understanding and what specifically can be done to improve. Delaying, neglecting, or being vague about progress damages the teacher-student relationship, as well as the final product indicating mastery of the standard.

The rapport you develop with students through conversation and observation demands the same level of respect, professionalism, and care when you respond to their work. Flippant remarks, sarcasm, and even some forms of criticism can be misunderstood and put a teacher in the uncomfortable situation of having to validate those comments to parents and administrators. Be as genuine, honest, and supportive as you are in person, and keep your comments on the skills and the content, not on the person.

If you are unsure of the best format for responding to a student, consider how the words will be best received and incorporated. Is it better to have a sit-down conference with a student about a piece of writing instead of composing marginal notes or end comments that might get overlooked? Where is the best place to compose your thoughts on a work submitted to you electronically?

One new option to experiment with is leaving an audio or video response as feedback. Within many online grading programs is a media-recording feature where you can leave students a message. Think of the advantages: Students are more likely to listen to and appreciate the tone of your voice speaking directly to their work's strengths and weaknesses, and you get to personalize the message affirming those things specifically. The time you may have previously invested in a carefully worded written response for each student can now be aimed at a more accurate and accessible verbal option.

Over time, you will learn what method students prefer and can respond accordingly. Perhaps the same rule applies for grading as it does for professional communication: Text back who texts you, write back to who writes to you, call back who calls you, and so on. The task itself will dictate what is best. A short written prompt like an exit slip may merit a few handwritten words in return. A lengthy multipage essay submitted online may be just the right work for some annotated marginal comments and an audio response in summary.

Experiment with feedback. Think about what you would find the most helpful and clear if you were the author or artist. Clarity is the objective, not whatever is going to save you time.

One more lesson to incorporate involving feedback to students: Never use the word *but*. Challenge yourself to correct a student's error without ever using that word. Whatever positive statement you build up before the conjunction gets instantly nullified or forgotten afterward. Develop the craft of providing personalized support and the results will be that much more impressive.

A STUDENT-CENTERED HOMEWORK POLICY

You have convinced students to attend your class every day and, once there, to engage in the activities aimed at improving their knowledge and showcasing their mastery and growth. The closing bell is about to ring, and the question about homework surfaces. Is what you are asking students to complete for an upcoming class session anchored to today's skills? Since students are quick to spot a fake, they can also see right through busywork. Instead of homework being a necessary evil of the system, how can you frame homework as a worthy extension activity and one worth their time?

First, any homework assigned in the last five minutes of the class period will quickly be ignored or forgotten. Do not take it personally; the timing was just off. Handing students a worksheet as they file out the door is a poor way to establish value for completing a task. If there is to be any intentional assigning of homework, mention it at the very beginning of class. Tease it at the outset, especially if the skills necessary to complete the task have not yet been covered. Try statements like these:

- "Tonight's homework will address these skills; though that means little to you now, it will make sense after today's class. Attend closely to see how this concept works in class, and I am confident you can do it again on your own at home."
- "If there is any homework tonight, it will be leftovers of today's activity that time did not allow us to complete. I am confident you can continue this on your own if that becomes necessary. Let's get started!"

When students realize their success on a given homework task requires attention to the day's instruction and activities, you already have won some buy-in. If students themselves created the activities or even the assignment itself, the buy-in increases. Somehow the association of homework being a dreaded chore diminishes the more it is connected to the day's learning, the unit objectives, and some intrinsic value. Homework for simple completion gets copied because the value is only "done-ness" and points. Homework for enrichment gets creative, yields a greater return from participants, and has longer-lasting benefits.

A LATE WORK POLICY YOU CAN LIVE WITH

Still using an archaic zero-tolerance policy for late work? Then just be sure you never do anything late in front of your students. Ever. Your credibility as a dictator hinges on your ability to remain consistently insensitive. Or you could consider a policy recognizing that students struggle with real-life issues that legitimately interfere with their ability to complete certain things on time. Just like everyone else, teachers included.

The student who didn't turn in her paper this morning spent the night in her mom's car (you didn't know), yet your policy sees past the necessity of training the academic skill and instead prevents the student from earning those valuable points. You know she can do it, but too bad, too late, move on, right? There is nothing student-centered about this. *Do you expect me to follow up on every missing assignment with every student?* you ask. Well, if the assignments are not busywork and are spread out because they have value, yes. Show you value people more than points and everything else will fall nicely into place.

Do not abandon your late policy entirely. Keep to some realistic real-world standards, of course, but also observe what may be causing the lateness. Work out a mutual plan with (not against) the student to remedy the fault and keep opportunities to demonstrate the skill at the forefront. You likely needed some remediation in your role as an evaluated instructor and have appealed for mercy for some lateness of your own on required paperwork. Have the same compassion when work comes in to you.

Establish a policy where students will receive no consequences on an assignment until after you have had a face-to-face conversation and reached an understanding about why the assignment was late. Don't be the teacher who says, "I know you were in the hospital, but you knew your paper was due online." Instead say, "Let's work out a plan for how you can show you have gained these essential skills."

If necessary, create a sliding scale where the assignment loses a percentage of value each day it is late. Stop at 50 percent and keep it there until the end of the grading period. Students should be able to demonstrate a skill at some value between ten days after the due date until the end of the term for at least half the credit. Separate behavior from academic skill. An instant zero just hours after a deadline communicates to the student that your assignment is more important than the person.

Do some U.S. citizens submit their income taxes after April 15? Yes, and with a penalty they are aware of and have accepted. Do you return all graded papers in a reasonable time? The grace you need is the grace you extend because the task, and the person performing it, has a value.

CHAPTER 4 FOOD FOR THOUGHT

Which interventions in your practice are truly student centered and which ones still need to be?

____

____

How can timely and accurate feedback enhance relationships, academic and social-emotional health, *and* mastery of the standard?

Why is it essential for students to know the purpose behind every task they perform?

This fed my thinking:

I am hungry to pursue or try:

Chapter Five

The Taste Test

Time to Assess Mastery

FROZEN, BOXED DINNERS VERSUS HOMEMADE

One joy of going to a nice restaurant for lasagna is trusting that the chef is not going to microwave an industrialized frozen dinner in a prepackaged, store-bought tray and then transfer it to your plate. Behind the handcrafted dish that makes its way to your table is thoughtful attention to the layers of pasta and cheeses, which takes talent, and an awareness of time and temperature for cooking, which takes training. Perhaps the lasagna can even be customized to your liking. Yes, please include the spinach, thank you.

How does a restaurant owner measure customer satisfaction? "Ask and observe," Kelly Herkert answers. "Part of customer service is checking to make sure everything from the food to the environment is satisfying. One time I asked a woman how her order was and she said, 'Good,' and I was thinking, *Is 'good' bad or is it excellent? How can we be better than 'good'?* I don't put much stock in online comments, but ignoring them completely could also be bad. When customers walk away, I want them to be as happy as possible."

Brian Herkert enjoys the process of making his soups from scratch every morning. He has found his art and pours his passion into perfecting it. Years of experience, tasting, observation, and feedback continue to develop the product to exactly what customers will enjoy. Brian does not want his soup to taste like it came from a can or a restaurant; he wants it to taste like home. When a customer feels at home, it is because his or her individual needs have been recognized and met.

In schools across America, assessments can feel canned and routine. Testing is a recurring experience that students are used to, but how often are their individual needs taken into consideration when the test is not a national, standardized one? Assessments for any general content area are easy to find in workbooks, online test generators, or even the archive of file cabinets from previous instructors. None of these documents, however, know the students sitting in front of you today.

In order to identify to what extent students have achieved mastery of the skills you have introduced, especially if they have participated in lesson creation and implementation, let students get involved in the assessment process as well.

DIFFERENTIATION THRIVES HERE TOO

All tests come down to a core skill of being able to read, whether that includes directions, prompts, problems, or passages. Literacy matters in this experience whether the content is written, heard, numerical, or artistic. Have students in each course throughout the building been thoroughly trained to be literate in the subject area before an assessment occurs? Since each teacher in the building is, in a sense, a literacy coach, the answer should be yes.

The reading demands that students encounter in one class are not the same as in the next. In a given day of five core classes, students might need five different approaches to text. Are they equipped to engage and unlock each challenge? Sure, they may be discussing a nonfiction article in sophomore English, but the black-and-white photo in the cultures class slide show can't be "read" the same way. Then an hour later, students might be following directions for a chemistry lab or translating a conversation in French II.

One step toward understanding disciplinary literacy and using this perspective to create a student-centered class assessment is recognizing that reading skills do not transfer wholly from one course, genre, or format to the next.

If teachers are to address diversity in the reading material to help students experience success across disciplines, is the same happening for reading assessments? If students benefit from varied opportunities to *gain* skills, shouldn't teachers also vary the methods through which students demonstrate to what degree they have *acquired* skills? As important as the variety in reading skills is for each unique scenario in a student's day, teachers must also consider the value of differentiating their *measurements* of reading comprehension.

BEFORE YOU CREATE AN ASSESSMENT

When the academic unit comes to the point where teachers need to assess the level of acquisition or mastery (formative or summative), consider these four important questions:

1. Has the student experience of accessing text throughout the unit been diverse? Paying attention to student responses to and engagement levels with reading prompts informs the decision of how each student reads best. Why stay in one mode of reading all the time, knowing this alienates a portion of the class?
2. Has the student experience of processing and reporting (writing/speaking) about the text been diverse? The opportunities students have to reflect and report on their reading of course content should be as diverse as the other phases of the process.
3. Will the student experience of demonstrating mastery of the *skills* (not content) be diverse? Single-moded testing is just as alienating and does not challenge students to acquire and attempt new skills.
4. Do students know the art of decoding questions for how to best answer them?

Developing a reader who previously struggled necessitates an understanding of the student's specific areas of difficulty and offers opportunities that sometimes challenge weaknesses and other times confirm strengths.

For example, if Andrea, a high school freshman, reads better when there is an audio version playing concurrently, then provide this accommodation. On alternate days, however, place Andrea in a reading group where the read-aloud is live and not recorded. On another day, give Andrea a chunk of time to read independently, followed by a penalty-free check for understanding. In a safe-risk environment, Andrea will accept the challenge and grow in her area(s) of weakness and still have days of strength to solidify her grasp of the text and the skills.

Do students get more than one way to access text within a learning unit? If the approach to unlocking, decoding, or encountering text is always the same (read to self, for example), how will the assessment results and lifelong skills and habits for students who struggle in this one method ever improve?

A companion piece to the actual reading is the follow-through. Do teachers have enough flexibility and awareness—think professional development and best-practice sharing—to give students multiple opportunities to process and report their questions and discoveries? If students are always writing short responses or completing rote fill-ins daily instead of conversing with others, where is the growth? If given the opportunity to create their own assessment, how many students would design a fill-in packet for themselves? None.

Packets do not teach, and completion does not always reflect total comprehension. The student whose mission is to find answers to simple questions will complete a worksheet for points. Once the transaction is complete, the student feels the obligation is over, and none of the supposed learning sticks. In the grade book, the assignment status registers as turned in, yet when it comes to a test of that same material, the skills will be lacking and a poor score will result. Why do teachers continually have to reconcile completion grades and low scores on tests? Because the two tasks of *fill this in* and *take this test* do not match in complexity.

Do assessments mirror the same diversity and level of challenge as the mid-unit activities? What do teachers and students really get to highlight if the measuring tool is *always* the same? Do not throw away all your scantrons since data collection on standards is necessary, but at the same time, be sure not to use them exclusively.

Knowing the content for a test is not a skill. Developing each student's area of weakness and confirming their strengths (and using them to mentor others) is the more noble aim of a diverse and student-centered classroom. Perhaps the best way to frame assessments in a specific discipline is through identifying and prioritizing the objective.

WHAT IS THE UNIT OBJECTIVE?

What will be the most valid and accurate indicator that true learning has occurred in your specific discipline? Since memorization is not an objective, toward what higher cognitive ability can students strive?

Daily learning objectives point to the course objective but must also pass the checkpoints of assessment and unit objectives to remain valid and measurable. Add a "Why?" statement to a daily target slide to help keep the *reason* for the day's activities in alignment with what skills students need to show mastery of at the end of the term. See figures 5.1 and 5.2 for examples.

How do you sell the value of your activities? How do you sell the value of your assessments? Proactively answer the "Why are we doing this?" question students want to ask (but often do not verbalize) before they engage in the day's plan.

With this clarity established in your class, students will know what strategies to use and how these differ from strategies used in other content areas. Teachers want students to recognize that the literacy tools for unlocking the meaning of a poem in English will not work for decoding the directions in algebra or deciphering the voice and audience in the chemistry lab safety video. Students need multiple tools for multiple reading tasks and repeated

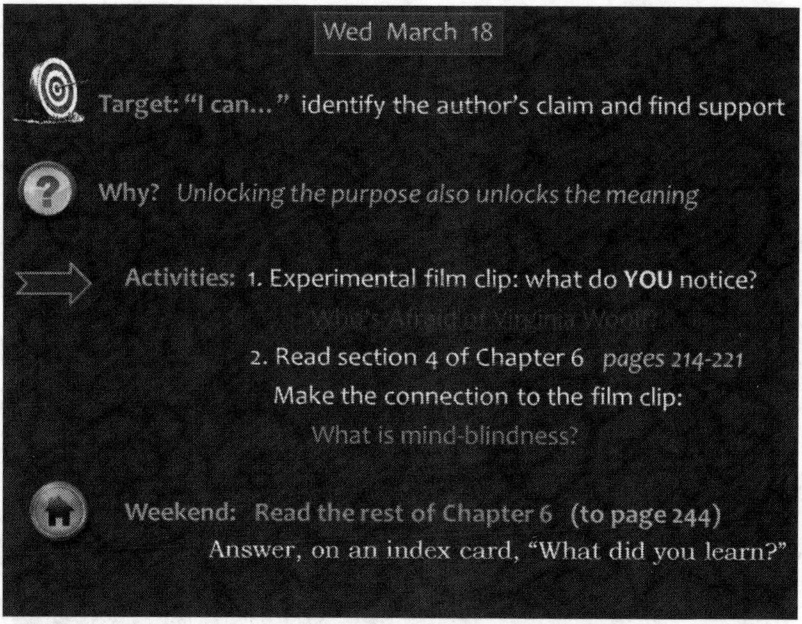

Figure 5.1. One sample of a daily target slide with a "Why?" statement. ***John M. Hayward***

practice to know which tool is best for which challenge. This too is disciplinary literacy.

DURING AN ASSESSMENT

An engaging component of assessment design is figuring out how to have students interact with the text or materials to arrive at conclusions and help them support claims *as part of* the testing experience. Composing their responses to higher-level thinking prompts will require access to the text and will help students be more college and career ready. In many English courses, for example, students are encouraged to read extended texts in order to build appreciation of them or to store the content in long-term memory. What about asking students to wrestle with the author's views and evaluate the author's craft? Is it acceptable for students to express their dislike of a text? In history, what are the test directions asking students to perform? Appreciation and memorization are *not* standards.

The methods students can use to interact with the text and demonstrate their understanding are as unique and diverse as your discipline. In your assessment rotation, students have several options:

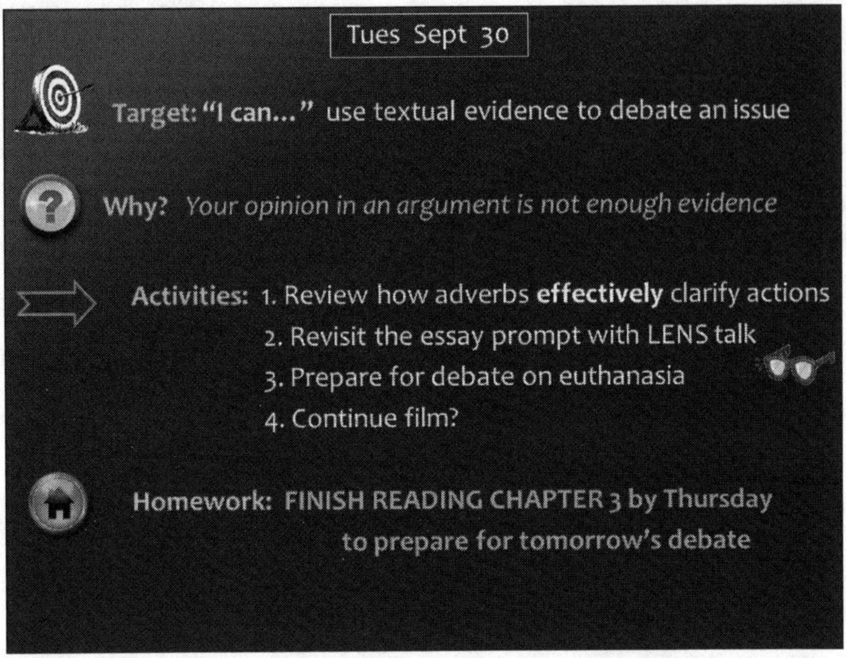

Figure 5.2. Another sample of a daily target slide with a "Why?" statement. ***John M. Hayward***

- Traditional testing format
- Performance
- Product
- Everyone answers in an open forum
- Observation
- Recording audio response (have students turn in their voice)

What methods did you use to become more familiar with your subject area? What skills can you be more transparent about using as you teach through examples?

Creating an assessment scenario where students depend on the text or an artifact enriches their awareness of audience, purpose, structure, tone, and so on. Worried about accountability? The student who did not prepare will still not be able to fluff his or her way through; you will know it and will be able to intervene accordingly.

Here is an unsettling thought: Has a student ever turned in a scantron at the end of a test and said, "Now I understand"? Usually the response from a student when tests have been graded is, "I got seven questions wrong." In this all-too-common scenario, did any authentic learning take place?

Do students know how to decode questions for the essential information requested? Without exposure to and practice with various question stems and techniques, students will struggle. Poor performance on exams is not always a reflection of not knowing the content. What if students who know the content and possess the skills struggle because of how the questions are asked? Teachers rarely want to admit that low scores are the fault of the test itself, but if the questions cannot be understood, then neither can the answers students formulate. Think about that for a minute. With all the options available for students to demonstrate mastery on a test, why was *this* one chosen?

How often in your specific discipline do students create their own rubric, grade themselves, or share the responsibility of grading others with you? Students experience greater investment and ownership of their learning, are more critical of their achievement, and learn proper methods of skill evaluation when they participate in the assessment process in roles beyond that of just the receiver. Make the invitation. Come to the table with your own nonnegotiables and seek input from students about how to make the measurement of skills accurate, fair, and complete. Begin the conversation by identifying what mastery of the unit standards looks like.

WHAT DOES MASTERY LOOK LIKE?

Before students can create a quality product, even if it is a performance, they should have opportunities to read, view, and evaluate samples at a variety of quality levels. Ask, "How many of you have learned something positive from someone else's negative example?" and an overwhelming majority of students will respond with stories of lessons learned from failure. Yes, there is value in using mentor texts and samples that earned an A for former students or texts that were published professionally. There is also much to gain in analyzing why a product in the C, D, or F range does not meet expectations.

Mastery is the repeated and consistent-quality demonstration of an acquired skill.

"Exceeds" = *Wow*
"Meets" = Yes
"Does not meet" = Almost (*failing forward*)
"Failure" = No evidence of skill acquisition (*yet aware of learning and ready to start anew*)

What are the models students are using to understand the expectations of quality? Someone looking to buy a car, for example, establishes what will qualify as acceptable in several categories, such as price, fuel efficiency, and reliability. Show students three different pictures of cars: a new one, a used one, and an abused one. Talk about quality and compromise and why certain criteria matter in a finished product. The same goes for the expectations we have for a unit of study. These are the expected skills, the activities we will use to acquire those skills, and the tools we will employ to indicate levels of mastery. Students are ready for assessment in any discipline when the process has been shared, clearly communicated, and addressed in a variety of ways. Keep in mind the following:

A student's answer to "*What* are you learning?" should be *skill* statements.
A teacher's answer to "*How* are you teaching them?" should be *content*.

AFTER THE ASSESSMENT

Three questions to ask at the end of the assessment:

1. What will students and teachers do with the data?
2. How will you address weaknesses in assessment results? (Why keep students in a perpetual mind-set of capped ability?)
3. In what ways can *everyone* celebrate? (Not just the A students)

If assessment data does not improve the instructional approach for upcoming units or clarify self-reflection, and if students themselves do not have a clearer picture of how to improve themselves, the entire unit has missed its target. Clarity and productive use of the results encourage all future investment in the process. Addressing the usefulness of assessment data is the key to avoiding shutdown and fostering growth instead.

Anything that helps students recognize how to overcome an area of weakness is a win. Within perpetual stagnancy, there is no victory. No one wants to utter or hear, "He will always be a B student." What can the student who earned a 78 percent on the assessment celebrate? Find the positive, and use that step to advance.

Process these four final thoughts about assessments:

1. Skill-based unit design helps everyone identify student strengths and weaknesses sooner.
2. Multiple and varied exposure to and manipulation of text or materials builds appreciation, comprehension, and retention.
3. Forced-choice answers do not stick with students as well as reasoned, communicated responses do.
4. Reading assessments that are text dependent and student owned best reflect skill regardless of the discipline.

CHAPTER 5 FOOD FOR THOUGHT

What can teachers do to enhance the quality, personalization, and accuracy of their assessments of student skills?

How can students play more of a role in the assessment process?

Why should testing be standardized sometimes and varied at other times?

This fed my thinking:

I am hungry to pursue or try:

Chapter Six

Keeping the Business (and the Shopkeeper) Afloat

The first major challenge for the Everdine's staff in Naperville came as early as the second day. Their marketing promoted images of the best grilled cheese sandwiches in town, made on thick-sliced bread. Whispers of their store opening and the good food offered on the menu spread through a word-of-mouth campaign among friends. Then an image-busting embarrassment occurred.

Kelly divulges the incident with a smile, thinking back on how awful it was: "We ran out of bread! We had to close our doors at two in the afternoon the day after opening because the response overwhelmed our supplies." An event that can now evoke a laugh forced the owners to seriously reconsider how they acquired and maintained their supplies.

"Our guests are what keep us alive, so we want them to be happy," Kelly says with a genuine sigh of relief of that moment having passed. Now they have a regular plan for keeping up their bread supply.

Has a teacher ever made a next-day change? Evaluation and readjustment are essential elements to surviving in the classroom. Read on for tips on how to stay afloat.

KEEPING ONESELF EQUIPPED AND REFRESHED

Teachers sometimes complain about their students not being engaged. The blank-faced, feet-dragging learners who may inhabit your school continually frustrate the instructors trying to reach them. *Why do they appear so lazy? Why are they too tired to bother getting materials for themselves?* Student fatigue is a reality that educators must address, and this chapter will do so, but first consider the image students have of their teachers. What do the adults in this environment look like, act like, from early morning through afternoon? Are the staff members in the building the best models of enthusiasm and engaged learning? This too can have a strong, yet hidden, impact on student morale and ultimately on their education.

Fortunately, there are solutions to student and staff apathy. Teaching is draining yet fulfilling at the same time. Balancing the drain and the fill is the art of an invested educator, and your students deserve the best you that you can offer.

If the morning alarm blends into yesterday's and your physical and mental fatigue convinces you there will be no relief, saying that you are not alone is of little comfort. In the day ahead, there has to be one shining moment, something you look forward to saying, hearing, doing, or even eating that will power you through the routine to get there.

Do you need a special coffee to get you to the classroom? Is it an egg morning? Should you break out your power shirt—the one that highlights your eye color? Did you pack the good leftovers for lunch? Did you stop yesterday's audiobook in a suspenseful place, leaving the big showdown for today's commute? If it is not the students, the colleagues, or the content that gets you excited and out the door, pick *something* to get the day started.

Maybe the routine needs to give. What if you changed the order of your morning, took a different route to work, ate a different breakfast? What risk are you taking in the classroom today that has you excited about possibilities? What new choice will students make today that they have not been offered before? The encouraging word (or perhaps an apology) you have been mentally composing for a while may be best aired today. That will certainly make today stand out as unique, won't it?

Refreshment is not as frequently delivered through the hands of others as it is self-served in this profession. In the restaurant model of education, the school serves the students, but who provides support to the servers? It's okay to wonder, *Where is the recognition? Why isn't my desk loaded with gift cards?* One key to survival is knowing how to treat yourself.

Can you power through a stack of grading without chocolate? You are one powerful, focused individual! The rest of the teachers in your building, particularly in the weeks without end before the next holiday, are craving respite and variety. Here are a few ways to discover and experience the benefits of renewal.

Talk to a Colleague

If you have not yet discovered the influence an optimist or a pessimist can have on your day, analyze the nature of the conversation the other person initiates. What starts out as a complaint, a rant, or a whisper may not be welcome or appropriate and will not relieve your stress and emotional burden; in fact, this kind of talk may add to it. Participating in such negative banter may feel like a release, but be careful of what this may do to your reputation as a trusted colleague and your image as a working professional.

Save your grittier venting for an off-site location and a nonworkplace confidant. If you must, talk generally about how to address behaviors, not about individuals. A student-minded instructor puts students at the center of *learning* targets, not dartboard targets.

An honest conversation about your concerns, without naming names or placing blame, is a great way to share ideas and invite feedback on upcoming plans. Professionalism invites reciprocation and healthy relationships grow as a result. Classroom practice, newly released resources, and the appropriate facets of your personal life should be the focus of workplace conversations. The open-door, sharing culture in which all teachers ideally thrive does not come into being without laying the groundwork of trusting comments, presence, and patience. Be the colleague you would want to turn to for help.

Joining an in-house or in-district professional learning community helps keep participants engaged in focused conversation and in the production of specific goals. Imagine the benefits of hearing perspectives from teachers outside your content area or building. Educators receive invites to professional development conferences all the time; what if you hosted one or attended one as a group?

Network with People You Do Not Know

Are you participating in a professional or recreational book club? This is a great way to converse about a topic of interest and grow yourself socially around a common activity. There are all sorts of benefits to reading! Consider organizing a no-hassle group in your school or district centered around one professional development topic each semester. Meet often enough to keep readers accountable but not so often that it intrudes on planning time or builds resistance. This should be the breath of fresh air you and your colleagues need to stay current on school-related concerns or the latest research.

Not enough colleagues interested? Join an online community of readers. Browse communities on Facebook, Twitter, or other social media focused around a book study. What a relief to know others can sympathize with your struggles and not judge. Enjoy the safe and candid conversations with the hope of knowing that someone's outside perspective may be just what you need—or that what you offer is just what someone else needs.

Join Twitter chats on topics in which you have an interest. Work your way up from an observer to a chat participant and even to a host someday. Attend area conferences, book signings, or other events likely to bring you in contact with others in your field. These interactions will keep your mind open to approaches you may not have considered and help you meet new friends whose joys and concerns mirror yours.

Reach Out to Parents and Volunteers

Try not to let the maverick pride of thinking you can do it all prevent you from reaching out to two of a school community's most valuable resources: parents and volunteers. These two groups of people are often thinking to themselves *I wish I could do more, if only someone would ask.* So be the person who asks! In the process of getting to know your students throughout the year, you also discover more about their support network. What talents and knowledge can parents bring to enhance your course learning objectives? What volunteer organizations in the community can partner with you to enhance the instructional methods you foresee?

Often the students themselves know these contacts best, so encourage them to make this pitch when they are outside of school. When students are aware of the unit goals and their learning plan, conversations with coaches, counselors, pastors, and others will reveal many more ideas previously untapped and unused. Bring a community together through the portal of your classroom. Feel intimidated? Get the support of your administration, with the focus on growing everyone and strengthening these connections for a greater good.

What contributions to your classroom can a local politician, historian, museum curator, librarian, or other professional offer? Ask! Open students' eyes to the world beyond your walls with a refreshing in-house field trip. If people cannot come to you, what can the advances in technology do to take your class there virtually?

The beneficiaries to the above ideas are you and your students. A refreshed and stress-free educator creates an environment conducive to learning and one in which students feel they can contribute safely. You owe this to yourself, first of all, and ultimately to the charges to which you have pledged commitment. Grow them and yourself at the same time, you teachable person you!

EQUIPPING FOR SURVIVAL

Do restaurants ever run out of saltshakers and have to order more? Patrons in need might pocket items like saltshakers and silverware, figuring the house can simply restock. Like pencils in the classroom mug, certain items tend to walk off to new homes. You would not hesitate to spend a little to make sure the customers have what they need. How much money do teachers spend out of pocket to equip their classrooms with materials necessary to support the learning environment?

Go ahead and sign up for that workshop. Sure, you will have to trust your class to a substitute and prepare activities for your absence (though students could be a great support here if they know your reason), but it will be worth it. You will come back refreshed and have plenty to share with students about the pros and cons of the sessions you attended. Would you dare be that transparent to students about being a professional who needs occasional refilling? Absolutely! Teachability is a great trait to model in the environment where you work.

Physical consumables are not the only valuable commodity in your closet or cabinet. Your strategy toolbox needs updating, especially the more you and your students empty it. Keep a table or bookshelf in your shared staff workroom full of professional development resources, books, or notes from seminars for others to browse. Consult this area for updates and encourage others to do the same. Maintain a web-based resource hub through the school's learning management system for teachers to access ideas and strategies. Upload what works for you; download what works for others.

ORGANIZATION AND TIME MANAGEMENT

In his quest to either arrive at moral perfection or identify how elusive such perfection was, Benjamin Franklin devised thirteen virtues. One of them was order, with the hope of letting everything have its place and each part of one's business have its time. Is perfect order possible? Classroom organization is only a start. If viewing posts on Pinterest for quick ideas on how to organize a learning space seems overwhelming, reach out to your more organized students, colleagues, or, yes, even a superorganized class parent.

Another benefit of giving students more control over their learning is modeling and releasing the responsibility of organization. Frustrated about handouts when it is time to collect papers—how some students go right to neat folders and other students have to start fishing through the depths of their backpacks? If you have not yet transitioned to electronic documents, submissions, and grading, have the talk with your students about organization and your expectations.

Ask students how many of them can walk a clear path from their bedroom door to their bed. Then ask how many of them have to kick a path to do the same. There is your gap. Organization has to be modeled and taught. Not a master in this area? Walk through the steps together! Transparency teaches amazingly well. Get folders, labels, and storage for your own files and show students the benefits. Declutter your desk, your room, and even your computer desktop in front of this audience, who will then begin to look at their own clutter and be inspired. Perhaps some student strategies can help you or others. Host a "life hack" day to which everyone can respond and get it done!

KEEPING A CLOSE INVESTMENT: THE BENEFITS OF A TWENTY-FOUR-HOUR TEACHER

A twenty-four-hour teacher has students, lessons, and resources on the mind at all times. While browsing the aisles of the grocery store: *Which item would make a great object lesson to illustrate the concept I am introducing this week?* While driving home: *What can I do differently to engage Jasmine, who seems to struggle at impromptu writing activities?* While watching television: *Whose leadership will direct Eric's group through tomorrow's activity since he will be out for a field trip?*

Having school always on your mind is not a bad thing—it shows you care. What creative idea you seek in the moment can afford to wait; because you are always thinking, you will surely recall it again later, or a better idea will come along, supplanting the first. Driving in the car becomes a welcome forum for meditative reflection and planning. Have an hour wait for an appointment or at a kid's practice? No worries—there is plenty to occupy your thoughts.

Ever had a student spy you at a store or an off-campus event? That is you, the twenty-four-hour teacher, defending your existence outside the classroom, acknowledging that you too do crazy things like drive, shop, and eat. Be proud of it; not everyone gets that celebrity status.

Teacher mode is also what makes your antennae tune in to opportunities to be the hero in public. You teach whenever you can. You organize where you see chaos. Even if you do not utter the words aloud, you silently correct the speech and writing of others. *Yes, that should have been an apostrophe on that sign back there. Ha!* You silently cheer for the cashier who calculates your exact change. Do not fight to separate from your school identity if productivity depends upon it. Be careful, though. Not knowing how and when to turn off your classroom persona can have its drawbacks.

KEEPING A SAFE DISTANCE: THE DRAWBACKS OF A TWENTY-FOUR-HOUR TEACHER

You cringe when people comment, usually with a poorly veiled sneer of jealousy on their face, that you get holidays and summers off. Regardless of how you explain that teachers pack twelve months of labor into nine months or that you have anywhere between twenty to more than one hundred students, it will still be lost on them, so don't even try. Well hidden is the reality that you are in high gear from mid-August to early June. This pace is often what makes or breaks beginning teachers, seasons the middle years, and wears down the nearly retired. Survival depends upon knowing when and how to downshift.

School administrators can help morale through incentives and activities. One idea is to give teachers a competitive drive toward a goal. A weeklong dress-down theme with daily tallies helps teachers loosen up a little bit and shows students the grown-ups know how to have fun too. Perhaps a fundraiser can inspire staff to get out of their comfort zone for a good cause. Dunk tank, anyone?

Encouraging teachers to observe each other is a great way to expose instructors, planners, and graders to fresh methods of delivery, class management, and organization. What incentive can you offer to not only recognize participants but also offer an outlet for sharing reflections afterward? Cross-disciplinary learning opportunities are the most rewarding for their perspective-changing newness. Think a language arts teacher can't learn something from a science teacher or vice versa? Try it and see!

Doldrums during the winter months? The cost of a roving hot chocolate and sweet treats cart will pay off warmly! Have a message to deliver to a department or instructional team? Conduct a lunch-and-learn session. Did you receive an invitation for an upcoming, engaging webinar? Host a viewing party in a conference room and snack and share your way through the takeaways afterward.

LIGHTEN UP

One sign that teachers are taking themselves too seriously is losing the ability to put the schoolbag down at the threshold and leave it there. Another is losing one's sense of humor, one's appetite, or worse, sleep. If you long for weekends to get more work done and then look forward to the week to escape from home, the imbalance has already begun. Right that ship with a redistribution of priorities, perhaps solaced by the thought that being at the top of your game occasionally means calling a time out.

When was the last time you took a walk, read a magazine article that *was not* about education, completed a puzzle? Part of the joy of getting out of bed in the morning might be the two-column checklist of what you can accomplish in a day, with the second column having nothing to do with school, family, chores, or errands. Losing sight of this simple and free escape ensnares even the best educators into becoming lifelong worriers and burden carriers. Exhaustion affects you and everyone you encounter, especially students, which is why it is imperative to be at your best.

BACK TO THE ISSUE OF STUDENT FATIGUE

You may have noticed that students are tired. They are not tuning you out *because* of you, so do not take it personally. Identify the reason for this fatigue. Perhaps the teenage boy who was five feet eight in August and now stoops to get into his desk is experiencing a growth spurt and needs more protein. Maybe Grace is not bored with today's lesson but has difficulty paying attention because her parents argued until two in the morning about finances.

When teachers take the time to get to know what is going on, even if only a few seconds' worth of investment listening or observing, those insights can help shape the instructional approach. "Just deal with it" is a mind-set many employ in the name of discipline to toughen students up for the challenge, yet this disregards the individual and his or her unique needs.

Is student fatigue the result of fifty-pound backpacks? Does one instructor after another in their day assign busywork? Are students employed or involved in extracurricular activities? This qualification doesn't earn anyone a free pass, but before the discipline kicks in to punish students, can an understanding be reached to help them balance their responsibilities? Teenagers do not always pursue or discover the solutions to demanding problems on their own nor do they come preloaded with methods for relieving stress. This is why some issues like tardiness, disorganization, and disrespect do not go away without some coaching along the way.

Be that coach.

WHAT ARE STUDENTS LOOKING FORWARD TO?

After the previously mentioned scenarios of poor student engagement have been ruled out, a teacher's class may just be boring. When convenience exclusively serves the server, something is out of balance. The first hint of a sigh or a yawn when students walk over the threshold indicates the dull-class sensor has activated and that something needs to change. This brings up the hardest issue of all in the move toward student-centered instruction and climate: sacrifice.

Teachers know which activities, handouts, and teaching topics are their favorites. Pet projects, idealized scenarios attempting to recapture former glories, and teacher-guided instruction under the banner of "I've always done it this way" are the hallmarks of a dangerous grip on teacher-centric planning. Sacrificing those moments to usher in student-centered potential can be terrifying. Yet what if this is exactly what today's students want, and what if this creates the conditions in which their most authentic learning takes place? Would you let your "classic" handout get in the way of that?

Tradition kills spontaneity. Without the input to direct their learning and the invitation to explore their thoughts, students become steered receivers into preplanned responses, and educators are happy to call it learning. It *looks* like effective instruction because students appear engaged and provide the correct responses, but the robots in this scenario have done no more than comply. Why would anyone look forward to that passive experience every day?

Look over your lesson plan or your agenda and identify how many learning opportunities students will actively perform. If class members do not physically move, talk, read to themselves, write, discover, take risks, and so forth, then how different are the students from the chairs they sit in? Your instructional-strategy toolbox has one more powerful option to exercise: looking for a new way to do what you have done before.

The goal for today's class, for example, is to read the passage and glean several takeaways. Something in this excerpt from the text is useful and meaningful for students' skill development. You have looked forward to this day because the opportunity to read this passage aloud reaffirms your love of this content. The richness and complexity of the language moves you and illustrates so many teachable things. Certainly, students will feel the same way when we are done. *Isn't that one of my hopes?* you say. You may have—once—considered letting students read it to themselves, but they would never go for that. What if they miss the main point? Your voice can do a better job. The wheel is better off in your hands, right? Welcome to the precipice of sacrifice.

Yes, you earned the college degree, but what if students did the planning or provided the materials? You found an article, but what if students found an article as well and the activity became a comparison to see which source is the most useful? You want to read aloud and guide students to the big idea, make it look like they discovered it for themselves. What if, through an engaging opportunity to read a *different* way, student conversations yielded multiple perspectives that included things even *you* had not considered? Collaboration, competition, shared ownership, new lesson design—these are the opportunities through which students can risk showing and sharing of themselves and reach conclusions previously unexplored. The hardest thing to do—letting go—will yield the greatest results and keep the business afloat.

EVERYONE AT HIS OR HER BEST YET STILL HUMAN

Even though it is hard to be formal in shorts, some teachers dress casually. It is hard to demand punctuality when you are late yourself, but sometimes it happens. Ultimately, we have to recognize that we are human and need to wear our faults like well-earned soup stains. The more often we can model an enduring and endearing spirit, the more likely others will respond in kind. There is nothing wrong with being a fallible human; students might appreciate that you are just like everyone else.

If wearing a tie or fancy shoes is not your style, do not do it. Be yourself. This goes with the trade-off of knowing students will be themselves as well, in their own coming-of-age quirkiness, and that an awesome, unique learning community will result. Blue hair, no hair, nose rings, glowing things, students will walk through that door in an array of presentations, discovering how to navigate their world. Show them how—not in an effort to make more people like you but to welcome them into a place where self-discovery is possible. Learn to enjoy this weird responsibility you have as facilitator; that is how you will survive.

CHAPTER 6 FOOD FOR THOUGHT

What efforts do you routinely employ to refresh yourself personally and professionally?

How can you connect all investors (students, parents, administrators, and community members) into a class culture-building team?

Why do some teachers experience burnout? Why do some teachers never change?

This fed my thinking:

I am hungry to pursue or try:

Chapter Seven

Celebrating

See? That Wasn't So Bad

YOU DID IT!

One reality of education is that those who put forth the most effort experience the most growth and lasting development. When teachers outwork the students, who records the achievement? If you solved all the problems, were students only spectators? A joyous benefit of a student-centered classroom is that the people reaping the most reward from their daily experience actually have the desire and vision to do so.

Daily involvement in class and the shift from receiver to creator mean so much for students—especially when their unique perspectives and concerns have a chance to be heard. A validated student gives; an underrecognized or ignored student shuts down. Celebrate the transition you have decided to make to a new, student-centered approach!

Despite the sacrifice you made letting go of your previous place of comfort, you will discover that this model of teaching comes closer to meeting the needs of today's students. If students are not tuned in to you when they should be, then reaching students where they learn and achieve best becomes your priority. Completing the shift from teacher-centric to student-focused learning experiences is a doable mission. Insisting on complete control no longer instructs effectively; surrendering to shared ownership means victory here.

Truly, what is there to celebrate if the only one smiling is the teacher and everyone else is miserable? Each person in the class deserves the right to feel festive and successful, regardless of the size of the gain. The cackle of superiority in the dominating teacher's laugh is as old as the movies they appear in, so leave that model in the past.

On any given day in your classroom, you may have students whose goals are not about getting an A on the test but are more about surviving. What are the learning challenges *each* student faces, and what can you do to help? Helping and making a difference are two of the top motivators for entering the teaching profession. What are students' battles, and how can you get to know what is involved? Most important, when scores indicate each student's level of mastery, what will each one have to celebrate?

Excluding students from hope hurts emotionally and fosters resentment. Sure, some setbacks can inspire resilience and determination, but *continual* failure creates a dangerous pattern and way of thinking. Break that culture through celebrations for which everyone qualifies to some degree. This not a "trophy for every kid" scenario; think of it as ensuring each student can identify a positive among the negatives. That foundation of encouragement provides the platform for the next effort.

WHAT IS THERE TO SMILE ABOUT?

After a test or a quiz or even when returning a project or an essay, what is one positive thing in your feedback as an instructor that each student will have to reflect upon? How can you make a C feel like an encouraging mark of improving status? What will you say to the B student who just earned a 68 percent that will communicate your support and not your criticism? Be real when you need to, constructive when you know it will be well received, and let each student know grades are temporary measurements of an ever-changing ability.

As the class grader, you are really nothing more than a bank teller reflecting a balance. You can't negotiate or sweet-talk your way to raising the balance in your bank account; you have to make more deposits. Academic points are the same way. Grades reflect what students have earned, not what you have decided upon, yet teachers often get the blame (and the bribes) for where scores lie. When both parties have a clear understanding of how mastery gets assessed and measured, fewer disputes will surface. If there is always something positive to recognize in the work students produce, what disputes could remain?

After you have celebrated at the student level, move up to the class level. What publicity can you provide for what good things are going on in your room? Where do you publish the results of student breakthroughs and discoveries? Do you have a class website, newsletter, or Twitter account? Let the school and the local community know what great things your students have done and they will continue doing them.

Speaking of community, now that you have made strong connections with parents and volunteers, how can you use these same channels to say thanks? Have students express their appreciation with a showcase of how the influence of community members helped them reach their goals. Did a community leader provide some help on a research project? Publish the results!

Celebration and recognition is something people love to receive when it is special (think rare, annual, or not routine) and authentic (not cliché).

TREAT YOURSELF NICELY TOO

Respecting your successes and failures will help ensure your longevity in this career. If you want to avoid burnout, remember to walk away each day with some nugget of goodness, a thought, a sound byte, or a success upon which you can reflect and smile. Maybe the refreshing coffee you missed in the morning rush can become the rewarding cappuccino in the afternoon. Whatever it is, you need to be good to yourself and not beat yourself up over frustrations beyond your control. You did not permanently damage anything or anyone. Tomorrow is another chance to shine brighter than today.

The copier jammed this morning and the handout you stayed up late to prepare did not make it into students' hands. You adjusted your lesson using a hastily checked-out document camera from the library and directed students to make their own copies of a few items. At the end of the day, you could be mad at the copier, mad at whoever came up with the standards, or even mad at yourself for not having made the copies the day before when you should have completed the handout anyway. You can't change any of that, so let it go.

Celebrate that you communicated the content of and reason for the lesson, that your revised plan resulted in some success when students took ownership of it, that the library even had a machine to check out in your hasty scramble, and that you didn't have a walk-in observation today. See? An easy change of perspective can clear your head of needless worry and move you forward to improving tomorrow.

All wait staff deserve a break, and teaching is a customer-service industry. Think about it: On your feet most of the day tending to the needs of people who have trouble controlling themselves decently while you try to get quality things done on time. (Go ahead, you may laugh at that.) The restaurant parallel fits rather well here. As you move from table to table making sure your patrons' needs are met, consider how fortunate you are to be in this field and to be trusted with this opportunity to serve. Cherish and celebrate this role you have to make such a difference.

CHAPTER 7 FOOD FOR THOUGHT

What steps remain in your journey from teacher-centered to student-centered instruction?

____
____
____
____
____

How can you academically and emotionally support a D or F student and keep the focus on improvement?

____
____
____
____
____

Why should celebration remain an essential ingredient in one's recipe for success?

____
____
____
____
____

This fed my thinking:

____
____
____

I am hungry to pursue or try:

____
____
____

Chapter Eight

Closing Time

Leaving One Year behind and Looking ahead to Another

WHAT DO RESTAURANTS DO AT CLOSING TIME?

You want to answer, "Lock the door!" Sure, there is a sigh of relief as the nine-month endurathon of teaching, planning, and grading efforts come to a welcome close, but before you fully embrace that sense of closure, it helps to reflect. What went well? What needs to be developed for greater effect next time? In what ways can students play an even greater part in their own education?

Like any good playdate coming to an end, it's time to put the toys away. During cleanup, summarize evaluation lists and reflections throughout the school year of what worked and what should be revised, what should be preserved, and what should be tossed or donated. Convinced you will never use it again? Do not store it; give it away to an organization that can repurpose it. Not sure if you will use it again? Store it in the back of your closet or cabinet. Certain this will be an annual supply need? Store it in the front—perhaps even in an August to June order.

For each item you tidy up, think about its usefulness in the greater scheme of reaching students where they learn best. No need to keep more than two of any extra handouts you find (one to keep for future copies and one to share or file elsewhere), so create a pile for the recycling bin. If you have tests or sensitive papers, conceal them until they can be shredded or recycled at home.

Each desk and each chair reminds you of the conversations had in this room over the thirty-six or so weeks of the school year. Remember how nervous Gavin was to give his speech in October until Kari leaned forward in the seat behind him and whispered, "You got this"? Everyone still talks about the moment when, with dry-erase marker all over his hands, Sergio stepped back from the whiteboard, shouted, "I got it!" and revealed his answer. He knocked over a desk in the process of exclaiming how hard that formula was to master, but you treasure that disruption. How awesome was it that Emma finally learned how to incorporate the reading of marginalia in the class text? "I thought that was just extra stuff we could skip," she confessed. Now she knows better, and it happened right here in your room.

Even your own desk, though you rarely sat in it, brings you to reminisce about how many times you didn't get to sit down until the end of the day. Okay, so you had to replace the stapler, but at least no one found your stash of chocolate in the back of the second drawer. This vantage point makes you smile because it reminds you of the awesome responsibility you have as an instructional leader. You are thankful because your students outdid even their own expectations. Sure, there are things to work on next year (and there *will* be a next year, you have decided), but you will begin that preparation later. For now, you reflect and savor.

Have you given diners the choice and satisfaction they came hoping to experience? Were the fears with which students entered on the first day addressed and tempered? How many unscripted life lessons emerged through the conversations your safe learning environment helped create? These are the moments worth lingering upon as you close out the school year. The frustrations and failures were a natural part of the journey and only minimally affected the results. You put relationships first and have no regrets for doing so.

Kelly Herkert, cofounder of Everdine's Grilled Cheese Company, reflects upon how the opening day of a business is very much like the start of a school year. "We're just going to continue to grow and become more efficient and do what we can to make customers happy," she says. Failure to grow is tragic but not the end; failure to *want* to grow is worse.

One of the last tasks the Herkerts addressed before welcoming patrons, though it is a primary element of a restaurant's health and longevity, was staffing. "You can't hire staff and then have nothing for them to do, so we conducted a week of training about a week and a half before opening," Kelly says. Just as teachers do, restaurant staff members undergo performance reviews, including detailed observations about their role.

"Evaluations also focus on what staff are doing well and then what I can do better," Kelly says about this critical part of the business. "Christine, for example, shared some ideas from her perspective that I had not seen. I thought, that's brilliant, why didn't I think of that?"

Kelly asks customers as they are wrapping up their experience, "How can we improve?" Criticism sometimes comes, but she welcomes the feedback because she knows that is the only way to grow. Simply asking, "How was the meal?" could reveal short answers like great, good, or okay. Taking a risk to invite open responses, even if anonymous, proves its worth.

What procedures will students have for reflecting on and evaluating the semester or school year? Have you created a final exit piece? An entry slip on day one bookended with an exit slip on the last day gives students an intriguing look at how far they have come in such a short time. The appendix of this book includes forms and reflection surveys to use as bookends to a semester or school year.

Ask students to revisit their goal statements from the beginning of the term or the year and to be straightforward about their successes and struggles. You will have made it clear in your directions "I will wait to read my copy of these until after grades are posted" so that students are as transparent as possible.

Take any review of your teaching seriously, whether positive or negative in nature, because this level of honesty does not come from an administrator's one-day visit. The people who can help you sharpen your craft have been with you every day. Student standards for and expectations of good teaching have been finely tuned from years of educators across many disciplines, degree programs, and strategic approaches. Students may not always know what they need, but they are very clear about what they expect.

Do not aim to be their favorite teacher; be their most effective. Better to be productive than popular; better compassionate and creative than just plain cool. This data from students will inform a valuable portion of what you aim to do differently next year.

BREAKING TRENDS ON DROPOUT AND TURNOVER

With such a high turnover rate among teachers in their first years, what will you do to break that trend? Even if you are a seasoned veteran, what can you do to mentor a spirit of resiliency and love for teaching among your colleagues? With a dropout rate among students still a disappointing reality, what will you do to address their retention and interest in school? How did you rekindle the fading flame of interest when even you began to sour? Demonstrate your care for your profession in full display of its ups and downs. Show others how to cope.

A need for the enduring and equipping tips from chapter 6 can occur at any time. August is not your only do-over window (though it is more convenient). Each new day is a chance to refresh and retool your practice. Becoming a more central part of their learning experience is something students *want*. So if you happen to make a turnabout on a Tuesday in November because a teacher-centered approach has run out of steam, then let the change happen.

The rest of your year will be that much deeper, engaging, rewarding, and noticeably improved.

DIFFICULT BUT TOTALLY WORTH IT

You went into this business to make a difference, to offer something else than other brands offering a similar product. Something in your process and delivery will be better than the others, you said. Okay, there is even some internal competition, but what thriving field is devoid of competition? Yet you would not hesitate to help a colleague in a district or state other than your own. Every year you attend the same conventions as other teachers and have equal motivation to develop yourself as a professional, so why let pride prevent you from growing and networking with others? Be yourself, do your best, and bring willing people with you on the journey as you join others on theirs.

Your stiffest competition—whose strength increases with each innovation—comes from the things dividing your students' attention. The battle to win and keep your audience fatigues and frustrates you the most, yet you realize that your investment is still worth it in spite of this. Are you going to lose it because a fidget spinner threatens your class environment? Be bigger than that and find a way to incorporate what you cannot eliminate. Are cell phones an issue in your class? Weave their use into information gathering and they become a tool. The quickest way to validate a subversive trend is to threaten to be against it; the best way to kill a negative trend is to make it cool for your own use or prove it is obsolete.

Have you noticed some stores have apartments above them? Is that where the owner lives, struggling with the separation between work and home? No wonder students often believe their teachers live at the school. Seeing you in public is weird for them; it is shocking to see you out of context. "You don't live here at school, do you?" Okay, so maybe you have food there, a change of clothes, and may have, in a desperate moment, even spent the night. Brian Herkert spent a few nights in the back of the restaurant in the early days to keep up. The hours you log on the work site comes a close second to time at home. Why? Because you want to stay ahead.

That drive you have to get things done is contagious to students who need to see multiple models of ambition, yet this is simultaneously unfair to them. When teachers do not involve their students in the creation, implementation, evaluation, and remaking of daily learning opportunities, everyone suffers.

Enough late nights and bad dreams! Student-centered practices serve and benefit everyone involved. Clients have walked in the door with high expectations and a sense of adventure. Take the risk! Open the floor plan, the lesson plan, the grade book, and the content map with a focus on the people and the standards. Let go of the "from me to you" teaching model in order to embrace a more hands-on and relationship-focused approach. Determine that the students on your roster will do more than receive their education; they will live it. And when they live it, they will remember it for a lifetime.

ARE YOU STUDENT CENTERED?

As early as tomorrow, your teaching can be reset and your students set free. They will continue to be lifelong learners and will remember these transformative moments of choice and growth wherever they go. The more "relationship first" class environments teachers can create for the successive grades of a student's experience in education the better. You benefit from this, of course, but you did it for them. This work, this sacrifice, was always for the customer. Though you don't count your losses and profits until the day is done, you smile, because no matter what the record book says, you still made a positive difference.

You begin to see things differently in your school. You notice the people with their dreams and their faults and fears, their tragedies and triumphs, and you seek out their stories. You do what you can to reach them and help them discover and amplify their voices instead of your own. No one watches your classroom clock, willing the bell to ring out of frustration anymore. Insightful moments are more frequent and linger longer.

As each session concludes, satisfied customers file past you, chatting pleasantly about their experience. They are eager to come back soon. With less work to do than you did in the past, you will be rested and ready to greet them when you open your door again in the morning.

CHAPTER 8 FOOD FOR THOUGHT

What are you letting go of in order to create a more student-centered class?

____
____
____
____
____

How would your students answer this question if you asked it every day: "What are you looking forward to coming back for tomorrow?"

____
____
____
____

Why are goal setting and reflection both valuable parts of growth for students and teachers?

This fed my thinking:

I am hungry to pursue or try:

Appendix

Forms and Reflection Surveys

To get to know student strengths and weakness, likes and fears, demands and goals, it is best to simply ask. Beginning when they walk in on the first day to the last day right before they leave, give students multiple, safe outlets to be open and honest about their progress. The grade book will never reflect the whole student. A more complete picture develops when their own freely expressed words are part of the data gathering. Some of the forms that follow are part of my professional goal to have students conduct more self-reflections. Start with day one.

A first-day survey needs to be framed as a private exchange of information between the teacher and student only. This will not be shared aloud and will only be used to help you, the instructional coach, help them, the instructional athletes in training, develop into their personal best throughout the academic term. Refer to these answers often to be sure you have not overlooked something they have confided in you and hopefully incorporate students' answers into your interactions with them.

If a student writes, "Please do not call me out for being wrong. I am still jittery in class from incidents in seventh grade when my teacher shamed students for guessing incorrectly," then find safer, less-intimidating ways to include this student in class discussions.

If a student shares, "My father committed suicide two years ago this March. If we read or watch anything in class related to the topic of suicide, I would like to know in advance so I can be excused for that portion and meet with my counselor. Thank you," then do your best to support this child's emotional well-being. A trusting environment builds upon such knowledge.

At your open house, consider a short form for parents to complete, with a few candid questions about what they believe you should know about their child that no other data can reflect. You will gain insights students themselves may not have shared and get a glimpse of the extent to which this support network trusts you. Parents are curious about the content and assessments, certainly, but they also want to know their child is in good hands socially and emotionally. Show you care by asking parents to know more about their children as learners and as still-fragile people in development.

A student with opportunities to self-reflect begins to recognize the value of looking within and assessing the improvements taking place. Teens conduct plenty of outward comparisons to others. Dare them to be honest about their own progress toward personal and academic goals as it relates to your coursework. To what extent—perhaps asking every four weeks—have students closed the gap between their August realities and their May goals? Even a one-sentence self-reflection statement at the end of an assessment, project, or essay could help students see, in their own words, what more could be done to improve.

What if students led themselves to the honest conclusion that they could have prepared more for the speech they just gave in front of the room? If students annotated their math problems with a running commentary of why they made particular calculations, would they master those processes sooner?

As part of the professional evaluation process, teachers are asked to reflect upon the success or challenge of a particular lesson. Why not students? Really, it is as simple as asking. The following forms are just a small sample of what is possible for collecting these valuable insights. Know your audience and customize some forms of your own.

MR. HAYWARD'S OPENING DAY QUESTIONS

Take attendance Z to A. What name do you prefer?
I will ask you a question; then you ask me a question.

1. What kind of ice cream best describes your personality?
2. What is your favorite article of clothing? Why?
3. What will be your eventual claim to fame? For what will you be best known?
4. Create a new American greeting instead of shaking hands.
5. What would be your favorite meal after a long, hot day?
6. What is the worst-smelling place you have been to?
7. What is the hardest thing for you to throw away?
8. What is the coolest thing you have ever found?
9. If you could launch an angry tirade at any person in the news, what would you say to whom?
10. If you could housebreak it, what would make the best pet?
11. What is something you wished for silently that actually came true?
12. Who do you need to write a thank-you letter to . . . but you haven't?
13. Describe a vivid dream that changed the way you act or think.
14. If you could pick two celebrity adopted parents for a week, who would they be?
15. Describe your real or imaginary happy place.
16. What new menu item would you suggest for the school cafeteria?
17. August needs a new national holiday. What is your suggestion?
18. Invent a new Olympic sport—winter or summer games.
19. Describe the last time you saw somebody do something nice for a stranger.
20. What invention would make life easier or more convenient?
21. What is the most beautiful nature scene you have ever observed?
22. With an unlimited budget, what would you drive?
23. What is the most creative commercial or advertisement you've ever seen or heard?
24. Name the ingredients of a fun new breakfast cereal.
25. Describe a time when time itself moved really slow, or really fast, for you.
26. Describe an awkward moment of drama you have observed in a store.
27. Describe a bad haircut or other embarrassing moment.
28. If you were president for a day and could pass two laws, what would you enact or change?
29. If you had five minutes of radio airtime to the whole nation, what would you say or play?
30. Whose biography/life story should everyone know about?

31. What video game should everyone have played and loved by now . . . and why?
32. How would you entertain yourself on an eight-hour trip (other than sleeping)?
33. What is one fear you wish you could get over?
34. What is one fun thing you don't get to do anymore?
35. In what awesome way did you prove someone else's assumptions about you wrong?

ENG 1 Name: ______________________ Class Period: ______

FIRST DAY!

Today is my first day at NCHS, and I am feeling ___________. I woke up this morning and I ____. Today, I just hope to ____. I still have concerns about ____, but am confident about ____. At Central, I want to know more about ____________________________, and might get involved in _________________, _________________, or _________________. My best subject is definitely _________________, and I will try harder at my most challenging subject, _________________. My summer was ______________. One thing I will always remember about this past summer is ____. The last good book I read was __________________________. This summer, I also saw the movie _______________________. The song in my head right now is "____________________________" by _________________. My thoughts about this English class, specifically, are ________________. I think writing is ____ and reading is ____. I will probably need the most help with ____________________________. This year is going to be better! My goal is to _______________________ ____.

ENG 101 First Day Survey Name: ________________

While I was preparing to come to class today, I was thinking . . .

What I want you to know about me first off is . . .

One of my academic strengths is:

. . . yet I could really use more help in this area where I still struggle:

Please *don't* do this (which other teachers have done before):

What I really expect and want *in* and *from* a teacher is . . .

Regarding *writing*, my thoughts are . . .

Regarding *reading*, my thoughts are . . .

I am involved in ______________ this semester, which requires _____ hours a week from me, so keep this in mind, please.

Outside of school, I also spend time _____________ and _______________.

Someday in the near future, I see myself ________________ because I want to go into ____.

You can help me, Mr. Hayward, because my goal for this class (other than to pass) is . . .

This semester is going to be great (!) because ________________________.

Would you rather . . . (circle your answers for each topic)

submit papers in hard copy	*or*	submit papers electronically		
read a book in print	*or*	read an e-book	*or*	listen to an audiobook
get your news from television	*or*	radio	*or*	mobile media
do you socialize through Facebook/ Twitter/Instagram	*or*	talk in person, face-to-face		

1. What about writing is challenging to you?

2. What about writing do you enjoy?

3. What lesson (or "aha!" moment) has had the most profound impact or improvement on what you write?
   I write so much better now because . . .

4. What is the most memorable piece of writing you have produced?
   a poem? a song? a letter? a story? an essay?

5. What kind of literature do you enjoy reading?

6. What is the last good thing you read?

7. One major goal for this semester:

PEER EDITING SELF-ASSESSMENT

I am _____% sure I can explain what an analysis of a character's traits is supposed to look like on paper.

I am _____% sure I can tell the difference between a strongly supported and a weakly supportive quote.

My final draft will demonstrate that I have learned these three things:

1. About writing . . .
2. About the play *Antigone* . . .
3. About women and/or leaders . . .

I would measure my contribution to today's proofreading process to be _____% because . . .

Today's activity did/did not work for me because . . .

What Difference Did Your Involvement Make Today?

I feel comfortable sharing with others in a small group.	True	False
Today, I listened more than I spoke.	True	False

From this data, I now see that . . .

____

I felt my greatest contribution to today's discussion was when I ____.

My classmate, ____________________, also said something I found intriguing: "____."

An area of strength for me in today's exercises was ____________________.

A weakness I would like to continue to develop is ____________________.

Name: __________________________ Date: ____________________

What Difference Did Your Involvement Make Today?

Today, my group read and discussed _____ (#) stories. The story that most intrigued me was by ________________ and was about ____________________________. For my own story, the best feedback/ input I received was from ____________________, who said: "____." As I head into the next phase of the story-writing process, I am looking forward to ____ yet still have concerns about ____.

Today, I gave _______%.

0 *25* *50* *75* *100*

and received _______%.

This data tells me that . . .

____.

Overall, I thought the activity was ________________________________.

Name: _______________________ Date: __________________

What Difference Did Your Involvement Make Today?

In my group, I played the role of a ________________________________.

I felt my greatest contribution was when I __________________________.

I would rank my *give* at _______% and my *receive* at _______%.

An area of strength for me in today's exercises was __________________.

A weakness I would like to continue to develop is ___________________.

Final thoughts on today's group work:

____

____

Name: ___________________________ Date: ____________________

EXIT PIECE: CREATIVE WRITING

Well, here it is, your last word. What do we do instead of a final exam? You leave here with a statement. Compose a multiparagraph growth statement that includes answers to all of the following:

Prompt: How do the universal meanings of the works in this course affect your view of the world? Furthermore, how do they confirm, qualify, defend, or challenge your beliefs? How have you grown as a writer in the last five months? What kind of writer are you now?

What did you learn about yourself? *(How you think . . . talk . . . live)*

From what you explained in the "Why are you taking this class?" prompt on the first day, what did you gain or not gain?

Please remain "self-reflective" in this piece—I am not asking for a critique (either positive or negative) of myself or the class. I want to hear about *you.*

English 101 End-of-Semester Reflection Piece Name: __________

In what ways do you believe you have grown as a writer? (*How has your writing changed from the first day of class to today?*)

Did you meet the course goals you set for yourself at the beginning?

What is the most outstanding thing you learned about English in this course? (about literature, grammar, or the writing process)

What is the most outstanding thing you learned about *yourself* through this course?

What are some ways this course and its content or activities could be improved?

What are some ways the teaching methods could be improved?

"If you teach this class again next year, you should . . ."

What are your goals for the next semester? After graduation?

Other closing thoughts . . .

One confession:

About the Author

After teaching high school English for twenty-one years, **John M. Hayward** accepted an exciting, newly created position offered to a few teachers in his district. He now serves a teacher-librarian in a suburban Chicago public high school, networking with colleagues to increase literacy and research programming. John also teaches college composition courses, which extends his love for helping readers and writers. A combination of graduate degrees in English and theology plus graduate work in education makes the perfect formula for his success, he says. When not listening to his wife's second-grade classroom concerns or shepherding five children through their developing stories, John may be exercising or reading. More likely, he is sitting at his desk writing and wondering how long it has been since he last read or exercised. John enjoys presenting at workshops and conferences on topics related to literacy and writing. This is his first book about education. Learn more at authorjohnhayward.com.